Who Am I?

MY JOURNEY OF
IDENTITY

MElodyBahr

Phil 3:13-14

MELODY BAHR

ISBN 978-1-64468-089-6 (Paperback)
ISBN 978-1-64468-090-2 (Digital)

Covenant Books, Inc.
11661 Hwy 707
Murrells Inlet, SC 29576
www.covenantbooks.com

To my children, grandchildren, and whole family.

CONTENTS

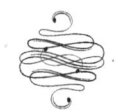

PREFACE

Identity is always a deeply personal question that others may ask or we may ask ourselves. Since society's way of identifying us much of the time is by our performance, they ask, "What do you do?" Some think this has to do with identity but it does not. "Where do you come from?" "Who are your ancestors?" These also do not speak to identity. They may talk about roots or locations but not who we are inside.

Here is a list of words that our culture might think or tell who I am:

Woman
Mother
Daughter
Sister
Grandmother
Aunt
Cousin
Texan (nineteen years in Iowa)
Teacher/state employee

Other labels they could use are:
Youngest and only girl
Molested
Sexually assaulted
From a broken home
Many close family deaths during childhood
Suicidal
Melancholy

Alone
Divorced
Single parent

All these describe experiences and events but do not tell you who I am. I used to believe they were the extent of my own identity. I thought that was who I was. It was pretty depressing and negative to me. No wonder that I accepted every one of them. Everyone around me did. Yes, I had gone through these events, but they in no way described who I am. In spite of all these things, this is who I truly am:

A much-loved child of God
Part of the Bride of Christ
A spiritual being that is growing and overcoming challenges
More than a conqueror
A listener to the impressions of the Voice of God
A fountain and channel of His Blessings to everyone
A worshiper
An intercessor
A joyful ambassador for my King

These are much more accurate about who I am on the inside now. It may appear that this is just for females. Not at all. *All* of us have lies and misconceptions about ourselves. We all have cages. Some we have made ourselves, some others put on us. Whatever age or gender, these truths about who we are apply.

I have recently been reminded that all these true "I am" statements are possible because of the Great I AM. Have you noticed that we can only say what we are by first saying God's name—I AM? Exodus 3:14–15 gives us the account of God revealing His own name to Moses:

> I AM, *that is who I am.* I AM *the God of the Living and the Dead who are not with you physically. That is My Name forever.* I AM.

I must speak His name before I say my own or anything about me because everything proceeds from Him. You may ask, "What about all that negative and hurtful stuff? Did that come from Him?" I can honestly say no.

Those things that I used to label myself early in my life were not from God because they were lies. Lies that I accepted and repeated to myself. I needed to be free from them. Yes, those things happened but they do not define me. I had to learn that what God says I am is what I truly am.

In this book, I will tell you about my journey out of darkness and into light—out of lies and into truth. It tells about who I know myself to be and who I am still becoming. When I go through challenges, He gives me the encouragement and provisions to overcome them.

This makes me stronger, and I get an upgrade in my being to face the next thing in my life. I have more victory and joy now because I have seen how faithful and trustworthy He has been in all the issues of my past. I am no longer under the circumstances. None of us has to be. Each one can find the victory and peace we long for in this life with The Father, Jesus Christ, and the Spirit as our loving family that guides us along.

This resource has been there forever. Open up and be changed. It is a lie that keeps us trapped and caged. It is the truth about God and ourselves that free us to love and enjoy life to the fullest.

ACKNOWLEDGMENTS

My first acknowledgment must be to my Lord. His is the One who has directed this work, start to finish.

Acknowledge and think of Him in all your ways
and He will smooth your path (Prov. 3:6).

There are certainly others whom the Lord has brought alongside me to assist in this effort. Four ladies in my church invested time and prayer in this effort, Melinda Gillen, Julie Wolber, Hannah Ritter, and Sylvia Neusch. Each of these ladies read and gave direction to the manuscript. They have laid up treasure in heaven by their precious sacrifice. I am so grateful for them all. I am blessed that they are in my life.

Others who have contributed toward this venture:

Sylvia Neusch, Barbara Lucchesi, Cheryl Moore, Nancy Khashou, Connie Conkle, Pat Ott, Donna and Steve Lyons, Carmilla Malgren, Shadya Williams, Ronnie Costello, Ken Sommerville, Bill and Sharlyne Crisp, Leslie St.Amour, Gail Wilhelm, and Saundra Bengston.

The cover design was created by Frank Conkle. Frank and I attended church together, and he was an excellent artist. I asked him to design a cover for this book, and he asked what my favorite colors were and what the name of my book was. I told him blue, green, and yellow and that the book was titled *Who Am I?* A few days later, he brought this cover to church, and I instantly felt connected to it and decided to use it as a cover. Frank has since graduated on to glory, and I feel incredibly honored to use his art as the cover for *Who Am I?*

INTRODUCTION

In my own growing and awareness of identity, Romans 5–8 has been instrumentally used. This knowledge and surrender to how God sees me has changed everything. It has aligned me to understanding who God is and how He views me and others. His opinion of me (and us) is the only opinion that matters because it's the only thing that is true and based in relentless love. To construct a strong and lasting building, it must have a firm foundation. This is what Romans 5–8 is. This is the foundation on which every upgrade of higher and deeper experience is built.

This is meant to be digested and fed on. Please do not just read through and put it aside. Take each part as a meal to be savored and enjoyed. Let each section be a guide to daily meditations. Think on these things throughout the day. Let them become a part of your DNA.

I have included Discussion Opportunities to facilitate exploration and conversation with God and others at the end of each sections. Let these be a catalyst to motivate your conversation with God. Be sure to listen—carefully.

When you have completed this guide through your identity, find other passages and whole books of scripture to digest in the same way. Let this process lead you in knowing how to feed yourself His Word and then feed others. The Spirit will be your teacher, and that means you only get truth. This guide is a genius at leading people into greater life. This *is* life; *choose it!*

I do most of my reading and studying of the Bible in the New English Bible (study edition, 1976). However, I have taken this translation as a guide and have paraphrased or modernized or just applied it more personally. This is what I would want for each of you who read and study the Bible. Make it personal—a custom fit.

These chapters follow the chapter divisions, and verses are grouped as paragraphs in the NEB text. I have used the same divisions.

Part 1

ROMANS 5

Verses 1–5

Since we are now justified by this faith, we are to continue in His peace. It is through Jesus that we are allowed to be in God's grace. We exult in the guarantee of the divine splendor that is ours. Beyond this, let us exult in our present sufferings because we know that challenges train us to endure. Endurance brings the evidence that we have passed the test. This evidence is the foundation of our hope. This hope is not trivial because God's love has inundated our inmost beings through the Spirit He has given us.

We are told that the divine splendor is ours. Because of this, we have the perspective that our present sufferings do not need to blow us out of the water. My view had always been that trials were bad and to be avoided or run from. "If I was good, I wouldn't have these problems." Well, that may be true to a certain extent. Certainly, if I'm the one who caused the problem by my own wrong choices then I shouldn't be surprised. But when things happen to us, we can realize that this is an opportunity for growing in strength and wisdom. Stamina, endurance, and confidence will grow as a result of overcoming an obstacle. This is something to go *through*, not camp out in.

This was a huge part of my own recovery process. By the lies, I believed and thought I was trapped and caged with no hope of anything else…ever. This hopelessness was constant and real. I managed a good facade but was dying inside. I had so much fear, anger, and death inside me. Occasionally it would erupt and overflow and surprise me and anyone around. Great energy was used to repress and suppress it back inside and keep it from blowing up again. It took so much of my life to hold it in and down. Blame and shame were what I had written on myself.

Everything was my fault because I was so evil and horrible. However, no matter how it felt, this was not who I was. I was deceived into thinking and agreeing with the lies that ran through my head. They were not the truth. The divine splendor is the truth about who and what I am. When I stopped arguing about my identity, I let go of all my proofs of worthlessness and accepted His truth about me. His view of me is much better, much more loving than mine. Why would I want to continue to believe lies that are so destructive? I thought I deserved that assessment. *But God* didn't. His love inundates me and proves how valuable and redeemable I am to Him. If He thinks this about me, why not just agree? I believed that He saw me as worthy until I could see it for myself.

Prayer

Thank You, Lord, for Your way which is the *best*! I accept Your promise because You are entirely trustworthy, and I will continue in peace. This is Your guarantee.

Verses 6–11

At the very time when we had no power to save ourselves, Jesus died for us and paid the price for us. We would hardly ever find anyone willing to die even for a good man. But Christ died for us while we were still in our lifestyles of rebelliousness. This is God's own proof of His love for us. Since we have been put in right standing—debts paid off—by His sacrificial death, we know for sure that we will be saved all the way to the end. So since we were reconciled while we were still enemies by His death, how much more shall we be saved by His life? And not just that! Now we have access to a relationship as dear children of God.

This is my identity. Not because of my past, but in spite of it, really. When Christ died for me, He knew exactly what He was getting. There was nothing hidden from Him about my condition. That's just how great His love is for me. He loves me just as I am but too much to leave me that way. This is how He sees me—debts paid in full. Nothing can keep me from this relationship. This is what I was born for. I am relentlessly loved, and I need to accept it.

For so long I thought that I had to earn this relationship. By thinking this way, I was believing that Jesus's sacrifice was not enough. There was something I had to do to deserve it. This was one of the bigger lies I had to let go of. Letting go of all the struggling and stress would seem to be a good thing, but I clung so tightly to the idea that this relationship would not happen if I didn't get my act together, and I had such a hard time doing that. Letting go of my own works and efforts was a big deal.

Trusting God who is absolutely trustworthy and dependable was a leap of faith. Being the one who has made that leap and landed securely on the other side, I can heartily encourage everyone that God is faithful and loving and more wonderful than we can imagine. He has taken my broken life and put it back together better than before and better than I had ever imagined.

Prayer

You thought of everything because of Your love for me. At the death of Jesus, every sin and every negative effect of sin was cancelled. I am free and clear. In that moment, everything that hindered my connection to You was removed.

From that time on Calvary, You see me as perfect and complete. I am in Christ, never to be taken away. I am there because You put me there. This is my position and my experience. I agree with Your plan and claim it as my own.

My own identity was clouded for so long. There were so many negative things I had accepted and believed. Some were told to me. Some were my childish interpretations of words or events around me. I grew up in a family of good intentions but much confusion. And there were things that were just not talked about even among family members. Truth and transparency were not part of the relational mix. These were people who loved God, followed as much of Jesus as they understood, read the Bible, served at very high levels in the church. They had a lot of information but not a lot of experience with a relational God. Don't get me wrong. They were doing the best with what they knew. They loved and sacrificed for others and touched many lives. I am proud of the legacy handed to me, but they had not shown me how my relationship with God could really be. I understood the rules, and I could quote scriptures and sing all the verses of the songs, but getting the necessary help to deal with important issues in my life was not there. It is only by His matchless grace that I survived through everything in my life to come to this point and finally know who I am and how He has always seen me. This delay was not God's fault. I agreed for so long with the lies, and it has taken a long time and loving people's help for me to step out of my darkness and into the Light that was there all along.

Verses 12–14

Listen to this! The first man brought in sin, and we have all followed, and death was the consequence that we all faced. Rebelliousness didn't need the Law to exist. It was here already. The justice code was already in us. We knew right from wrong. However, we still were under penalty of death for rebelling against God. But through what was foretold, God's Son came.

I followed and agreed with what I thought was true. I heard discouraging words often enough in my head. Others were positive and sometimes helpful, but I didn't receive any of it because I thought, *If they really knew me, they wouldn't like me or even want to be around me.* I didn't like being around myself. I was very judgmental, condemning, and negative about myself, but I worked really hard to maintain a facade of things being "just fine." I didn't talk to anyone about it. I didn't talk to God about it. I just spent incredible amounts of energy to suppress and repress the feelings of despair and inadequacy. I was constantly looking for approval from others. I would do good things really for the appreciation of people. I was not motivated in doing things for the delight of serving. I searched for love because I was blind to the love that was already there.

When I finally came to realize just how loved I was, everything changed. First, there was such a relief from all the effort I had put into keeping myself trapped in guilt and shame. Then, there was peace and love that flooded in to wash away all the darkness of my soul and let me experience the light of God's love *that was there all along*. I surrendered to it because I didn't have the energy to fight and argue with God anymore about who I am. I am who God says I am. I am a much-loved child of God. Better just accept it because it's true.

Prayer

The struggle between good and evil is in me, not God. There is no struggle in You. You always overcome. Right, justice, mercy, and grace always win! Let me accept and bask in the sweet surrender of Your victory. This was Your Plan—to overcome and share that victory with Your precious children.

You want children who are confident in who they are so they can enjoy all the limitless abundance of Your Spirit. I choose You!

Verses 15–17

God's act of grace so far outweighs the first act of rebellion. That one deed of wrong brought so many into separation from God, but its effect is vastly exceeded by God's grace and the gift of reconciliation brought by Jesus. This gift is so beyond comparison with sin. The judgement that followed Adam's act condemned us all, but the act of grace overshadowed innumerable misdeeds and brought acquittal to us all. Much more do we receive the greater measure of God's grace and right standing and have life and victory through the One Jesus Christ.

I fought for so long just to put one foot in front of the other. I went through times of wanting to end it all just so the pain would stop. I expended so much energy in keeping up appearances. I only fooled myself. Anyone with any wisdom or discernment saw right through it. I worked even harder around these people or avoided them all together. I believed the lie that it was all up to me. I couldn't count on or trust anyone. They didn't really care anyway.

There were a few people who cared, and I felt safe around them. They were the refreshing oasis in my desert. This was overwhelming. This is how deluded by the darkness I was. Then, little chinks and cracks began to appear as I was led to face fears and reality. My life did not completely implode because I wasn't spending so much energy to hide. More and more, light broke through and in. I had always thought light was there, but I didn't know how to get to it. I finally got so tired of the pain, and I just gave up. I stood in my kitchen doorway one day and said, "I'm going to get help, or I'm going to kill myself." I got help from God through people who loved me when I couldn't love myself.

What a relief to know that I was not alone, and that this life was more powerful than any darkness I had experienced. While I was in that hole, God still loved me and blessed me and provided for me. God is so much greater than what I had trapped myself in. There is no equality between light and dark. Light always conquers. God lifted me out of the miry clay and set me on a rock. He washed me clean with His Word, placed me in the position of right standing, and gave me a new song to sing (Ps. 40). The light is much more powerful. God doesn't force it on us but keeps on revealing it little by little to let us taste and see how good it can be.

Prayer

Hallelujah! That is the good news. The wrong was so bad, but the good is so much greater. They are *not* equal, not two sides of a coin, not like yin and yang. God, Your goodness is so much bigger and more powerful than anything. It's not a fair fight. I am more than a conqueror because You love me.

Verses 18–21

It is reasonable to accept that by one man, Adam, condemnation came in since we all follow that pattern. But by the act of another, Jesus, we are redeemed when we follow His example.

Many came under condemnation, but many are also freed. The Law came in just to confirm that we were law breakers. But as sin choices grew, God's grace became even greater. His grace is established in the generosity of His goodness and brings in eternal life through Jesus Christ.

I lived in self-condemnation and agreed with self-degradation for so many years. I believed in God. A relationship was begun with Jesus when I was seven. I knew God was around and that having a relationship with God was available and important...but I couldn't do it. I believed even more strongly in my unworthiness and sin even though I knew how badly I needed this union. I cut off access to it by my unbelief. I believed lies about myself and God. There were points along the way where I would hear some word or song or scripture that would break a piece out of the darkness I was in.

This is how God worked in me—a little bit at a time. As I got to middle age, there were starting to be large chucks of darkness and unbelief and distance from God that would fall off. Now, in more advanced age, I know freedom like I never knew before. How I wish that I had not fought so hard and long against the love and joy that was always available. I have forgiven myself and have left the past in the sea of forgetfulness. His grace is truly greater, stronger, more enduring, and magnificent than all the lies I ever believed. I feel so much more alive now than I ever did before. This was available all along. His grace kept revealing His love to me and never gave up on me no matter what.

Prayer

What a magnificent plan You have, Father! No matter what, You exceed all my failures and love me unconditionally. You teach and guide me not out of condemnation but out of love for my good. You are sooo good, Father! Keep pursuing me until I receive all that You have for me.

Discussion Opportunities

1.   What facade do you live behind?

2.   What are you still doing to earn His love?

3.   Are there any lies you are ready to renounce?

4.   Are you tired of fighting and arguing with God about who you are and who God is?

ROMANS 6

Verses 1–4

W hat do we say then? Shall we sin more so that there can be more grace? Certainly *not*! We died to sin, and so we are not comfortable living that way anymore. Don't you remember? When we identified with Christ in baptism, we went into His death. By immersion, we were buried with Him and *lay dead*! Then, just as Christ was raised from the dead in the glory of the Father, we also are raised to walk in a *new life*!

There are movies and TV shows about the walking dead. I've never been drawn to watch any of them, but I think I know the feeling. I can relate to the sense of being a shell of a person moving around with very little real life going on. Jesus had taken all the world's sin and every negative effect of it on Himself and paid the price for it all in His death. At a young age, I wanted and accepted Jesus into my life. I know the scripture says that His death was for me, but I didn't comprehend my identity in that death. Even when I was in seminary and took a class on the Gospel of John, we were shown that we died *with* Him and were buried *with* Him, I didn't get it. I was blind to the application of that reality to me.

Intellectually, I accepted this as truth, but I had no experiential knowledge of this for myself. I was a person walking around in grave clothes, in defeat, depression, and despair. I had given my best effort at doing life by myself and was failing miserably. I was just going through the motions of life while on the inside I was crying and screaming for relief. Yet, I would not let go of the despair so that I could have the relief. Pretty sick, huh? That was the point I came to in the doorway of my kitchen. "I must get help, or I'm going to kill myself." I didn't know until later, but that was all it took. I had to start to let go of my own efforts and release my strangle hold on death. I had held onto it because I believed I was supposed to. I believed the lie that misery was what God wanted for me. God wanted me to have Life, and the price was paid for me to have it. My own death would not free me but His did.

I have accepted that I died and was buried with Christ. Then, as He was raised by the power of the Spirit, so was I. Identification with Jesus's experience was what started my process of freedom on so many levels. This was His plan all along—my freedom. It would not be forced on me but would never leave me. God kept on loving and showing His faithfulness until I finally agreed and let go of the lies that were keeping me from all that was there for me.

Prayer

Hallelujah! All I had to do is say yes. I identify with You so that Your experience becomes my own. You are my model and example. I want to do everything like You as You did everything like the Father. My old nature and ways of seeing and doing things is *dead, dead, dead!* I have do overs because in You I have a new life. Yippee!

Verses 5–11

Here it is! We are thoroughly identified with and in Christ in His death and resurrection, just like Him. The person we were is dead, killed with Christ. It is dead, destroyed, no longer alive, no longer a slave, dead to being under the power or influence of sin. Since we died with Christ, we now live like He does, never gonna die again. We died as He died. We now live as He lives. Just like Jesus regards Himself as dead to sin and alive to God, we also, in the same way, are dead to sin and alive to God in togetherness with Christ.

I'm dead...certainly felt dead for so long. Dead and hopeless. My sins and their consequences ruled my life. My sins were not very overt. By human standards, not too bad. By Heaven's standards, I was full of pain, distress, and unbelief that anything could remedy this condition. I had been molested by a baby sitter's father when I was four and five years old. I had been sexually assaulted by a family member when I was twelve. I had volumes of misconceptions about myself, God, and others and add to the mix an undiagnosed and untreated PMS. Every month from the time I was twelve, I would go through the emotional roller coaster of believing that I was wicked, evil, and horrible. I spent the rest of the month trying diligently to hide the feelings of disgust and worthlessness. I was captive. I was a prisoner.

One of the things that Jesus said was His mission in life (Luke 4, reading from Isaiah 61) was to set captives free and release prisoners. Captives are those who have had things happen or done to them that have bound them up. Prisoners are people who have imprisoned themselves by their own actions, decisions, or words. I was both. I had things done and said to me, and I then agreed with them and said them to myself. It was a huge relief to really know and experience the freedom found in being released from condemnation. I learned that when Jesus died, He made it possible for me to die to sin also. Jesus, who had never sinned, willingly took all my sin and the world's and all the negative consequences of that pride and rebellion. It all died and became impotent in His sacrifice. Then, when the Spirit of God came back into His body, He was raised, having conquered sin and all its negativity. He paid the price for me and all of us so that we could not only be free of slavery to death but could have relationship with the Father just like Jesus has. Because he lives, I now live. Because He is raised and seated in heaven, so am I. That is where the Father has put me—in Christ. I didn't deserve it. God's love was the reason for all the effort to reunite all of us with Him.

Prayer

Yes! Thank You for this crystal-clear presentation of my position in Christ. Thank You that the old me is dead. It will not be washed up, dusted off, and reformed into being like Christ. It's dead. You have given me a whole new *me* born of the Spirit with newness of life. I am free from the power and consequences of the negativity of my sin and the enemy. You have put me in Christ so that is where I am. Praise the Lord!

This is shoutin' ground here! *Hallelujah!*

Verses 12–14

Sin and negativity no longer have the power to control us, forcing us to follow negative habits. We must no longer submit to destruction but follow the path to *life* like we have been raised from the dead. Let our bodies be tools for good, not evil. Sin's power has been broken. We are not under Law anymore but subject to God's grace.

Sin and all its negativity certainly controlled and held sway for a long time. This was my daily struggle. Occasionally, it demands attention but not like it used to. The dilemma before felt like fighting to keep my head above water. The more I stopped thinking that I could handle things by myself, the greater the rest and relief. Doing things this way with my own *gumption* (good southern word) wore me out. It didn't and still doesn't work. Accepting my own death to the controlling power of negativity and destruction is part of my salvation.

Realizing I did not and could not pull myself up out of the miry clay helps me finally see that choosing the victory that has already been won for me is the best choice. And it is my choice. I can choose death or life. Death is thinking that I know better than God. Life is knowing and accepting that God really has a better way. This certainly came up against my pride. But how was that working out for me anyway? Not so good. I could not pay the price for my own sins and mistakes. Jesus paid for me. Why couldn't I receive that? Lies of pride, unworthiness, and hopelessness kept me from that victory for so long. The way of freedom has been opened. Go on in!

Prayer

Yes, yes, yes! I'm *free!* You're *free!* We are all *free! Hallelujah!* I am on the path of life and joy and peace and truth because of You. I have first-class tickets for the journey that my Elder Brother paid for. And You have gone before me, preparing the way. Father, You own the path, and Spirit, You are the most brilliant guide. Let's *go!*

Verses 15–19

So what are we to say? Can we sin freely since we are under grace and not the Law? *Of course not!* You know perfectly well that you obey whichever master you choose. You are the slave of whomever you obey. If you choose rebellion, then death is the result, and there is no fellowship with God. If you choose righteousness, then life is the reward in its fullest and a loving relationship for eternity with God. Thank God that we were given the chance to make a different choice and leave the master of destruction and come to our senses to choose life and abundance. We get that abundance because of our wholehearted choice to follow His direction. We all once had yielded our beings to sin and rebellion, but now we choose uplifting victory, generosity, purity, and joy.

What a relief to realize I have a choice! Fog lifted and light dawned... I could make a new choice! I wasn't condemned to imprisonment. I could choose life and freedom. Me! Ha! I had the ability to choose. The lies that said I had no choices were the ones I had believed and lived by. *No more!* I get to choose. My choices began small, like testing the waters. For instance, well-meaning church people presented to me the lie that there is no more in the Spirit than what they knew. Their position was that this is all there is. They themselves didn't know all the *more* that was available in the power of the Spirit.

As a freshman in college, I broke from the "party line" and asked the Lord to give me the gift of tongues, a prayer language, and He did. The was a step out of darkness and lies. Also, being sent to Japan as an exchange student, my senior year of college opened me up to the realm of service and purpose. That year prepared me to let go of false beliefs about what I was here for and made me more open to His leadership. I had so thoroughly believed that God could not ever use me but I was wrong. God uses the weak to confound the wise and strong. He raises the lowly and exalts them about those who consider themselves so high. I have progressively gotten in deeper and deeper in relationship with God. Now I just plunge in! This is joy—the ability and even the responsibility to choose differently. This is freedom. If there were no choices, there would be no freedom. This is part of the good news—I can choose. It means renouncing the death and negativity that had been so familiar and comfortable. But did that existence bring any joy or happiness? *No!* Choosing life will certainly be unfamiliar at the start, but the benefits of freedom pay off immediately and then continue to expand and grow.

Piece after piece, my life started to feel the warmth of His light. Places in me that had been dark and hidden were transformed into spacious beauty. Not being bound up by condemnation and despair was totally new territory, and it had been available all along, just waiting for me to accept it. Of late, there has been an acceleration of growth and awareness. Understanding and Insight have increased. I am listening more closely than ever before, and I am receiving more direction and guidance than ever. This is available to everyone. I'm not unusual. This closeness and intimacy are here for all. Great and Mighty is our God, who can turn all our lives around if only we choose.

Prayer

This is my choice every day. I choose life. I choose You. I choose You because You first chose me. You made all this possible, and I am forever grateful. An eternity of my gratitude will only begin to demonstrate how thankful I am to You.

Verses 20–23

When we were slaves to sin, righteousness had no power over us. We only gained death in this arrangement. *But now* that we are free from the power of sin, we are fastened to God, and we gain eternal life. Sin pays what you have earned and that is death. *But God* freely gifts us with eternal life. We get this not because we deserve it but because He loves us just like He loves Jesus. We are incorporated in Him.

While I was still choosing to believe lies, my sin still had influence over me. But now that I have let go of the darkness and chosen light, I am no longer under its control. Yes, it's different. Yes, it's unfamiliar. Was what I was in so great? Did it really work for me? *No!* I existed but I didn't live the abundant life I was promised. I was the one keeping the promises from happening in my life because I chose to not believe and receive them. What child refuses to open their birthday or Christmas gifts? I'll let you answer that. That's how I was. *But God* kept on pursuing and cracking through my wall to try to get His love to me. Thank God He never gave up. He knew all there could be for me if I would just let go of death and cling to life.

His love is boundless and incredible, almost too good to be true. That's what the word *gospel* means. But the fact is, it is true and real. This relationship that Jesus sacrificed Himself to provide is more real than anything on earth. When everything has decayed and rusted away, His love will still be here. His love was the cause for all the efforts He made to get to me and all of us. We are now back in the intimacy He desired to have with us from the beginning.

Prayer

Lord, I want to be at home and settle in to this union with You. This is where life is. You have paid for my freedom. I finally agree with my release from the cage of my unbelief so that I can be connected to You more closely. This is Your free gift! I couldn't have paid enough to buy it. You have sweetly placed me in Christ. Help me grow into the vastness of Your kingdom and explore with You.

Discussion Opportunities

1. What will be different in your life if you reckon yourself dead to the old ways and alive only to His ways?

2. Who are you *really*?

3. What do you hold onto to justify being less than what He intends for you?

4. What about the "much more" of God attracts you?

ROMANS 7

Paul has written this letter to the Christians in Rome. Some of those Christians came from a Hebrew background. Some were Gentiles. In chapter 7, Paul specifically turns to the Jews concerning the obligations under Mosaic Law. Being a scholar of the scripture, it is understandable that he speaks to those who are wondering how the way of Christ fulfills all that they previously worked for under the Law. Chapter 7 is how Paul explains it to them.

Verses 1–6

Concerning those who know the Law, a person is subject to it as long as he lives and no longer. As an example, a woman is bound to her husband until he dies. She is then free from that Law. We have died to the Law by our identification with Christ, and we are no longer under the old Law. We have accepted the One who rose from the dead. This is how we will bear fruit and have evidence of His life in us. We used to go along with our lusts and appetites, which only lead us to destruction. *But now*, having died to that, we are free from that Law which leads to death and are free in the spirit to be all we were meant to be.

I am not of Jewish descent. The Law of Moses and all the traditions of the Jewish faith and culture were not evident in my upbringing. However, there was definitely a legalistic and religious interpretation prevalent in my family system. There were rules and expectations that were communicated but never talked about. One certainly knew and found out quickly if they had failed to meet the requirements. These were good people, and they did the best they could with what they knew. I know that they frequently felt they had failed to meet their own standards. They talked about grace, but I don't think they experienced very much of it. I grew up in that culture of rules and regulations and internally felt like an absolute failure no matter what I did. I did my best to be compliant on the outside, but internally I could not reconcile myself to the standard set before me. The fact is that was true. I could not reconcile myself and God knew it. This is why Jesus came so that I could be reconciled to the Father.

There was nothing I could do to be good enough to meet the standard of holiness that was required to have fellowship with God. This is why Jesus came and paid the price for me. He took on all my sin so that I could take on all His goodness. Jesus Christ completely immersed and identified Himself with my (our) condition. This accomplished so many things. Ultimately that opened a path to have a relationship with the Father that was His desire all along. Having accepted and taken on what Christ did, I am no longer under rules but truly under His grace. This has completely paid the price and opened the way for relationship with God.

Prayer

Thank You for making all this possible. Thank You for paying the price and enduring the shame. I am looking forward to all the joy. It feels so good to be dead to the power of sin and all its negativity and be totally alive to His life and freedom.

Verses 7–11

So is the Law equal to sin? *No!* But I no longer have the excuse of ignorance since the Law pointed it out. I would have not known that I shouldn't covet if the Law hadn't said, "Don't covet." Without the Law, sin is not realized. I would never have known I was breaking the Law without the Law present. The command which should have pointed me to life only revealed the death inside me. It was supposed to guide to life, but my choices turned it to death.

The culture of religious legalism is still very strong. We see evidence of it all over the world. These are people who are very comfortable in their cages of rules and regulations. Freedom is a fearful thing, first, because it is unfamiliar and, second, because they are not in control anymore. They may say, "But there's no safety net, no firm foundation." Yet, His grace is our safety and rock. The way of the Law says that if I follow these rules, then I have earned myself into heaven and a relationship with God. This is impossible. We cannot perfectly obey every Law.

Breaking the Law is what we all have done. Just having the pride that says I can do this for myself is breaking the Law because we are setting ourselves up as greater or equal to God. First commandment… broken. The Mosaic Law actually only pointed out how far I was off the mark. Every one of the commandments are for my good—to help me live well with God and others. But in my pride, they were turned to points of condemnation since I couldn't follow them perfectly. Left to myself, there is no hope. Left to the Law, I am condemned.

Thank God He didn't leave me there. His love was so great that He would do *anything* to make it possible for me to walk with Him, and He did! He did the only thing that could have had any effect on my situation—He sacrificed Himself to pay what I owed. He satisfied and fulfilled the debt my sin had created. I could do nothing. He did it all. And when it was paid, He said, "It is finished." Paid in full. Done deal. No more and nothing else to be done. This is the free gift I choose to accept. I don't deserve it and can't earn it. This was done *for* me. I receive it. I grasp it like a drowning person holds on to a life preserver. I take it and hold on. I put my trust in the One who pulls me to safety and life.

Prayer

You have overcome the enemy who so insidiously wants to turn good things against us. That power has been broken by the blood of Jesus. Now all things work together for our good.

Thank You that we are no longer helpless slaves to death. Thank You that You thought us worth saving. Thank You for loving us that much. *Hallelujah!*

Verses 12–13

The Law and commands were good in themselves. They did not bring death. Pride and the arrogance that we knew better than God's directions killed us and revealed the true colors of sin. The enemy used a good thing to entice us into death (like in Eden). We get to see just how destructive sin is.

The directions that God gave were not evil. They were meant for me to follow so that I could have a peaceful and good life. However, my pride thought I knew better. I thought I could earn my way into a better life by following my own way. What a crock! Who did I think I was? Really, who did I think I was? I accepted and believed the lies that I was wicked, evil, and unworthy, and that I had better work really hard to earn God's love. I couldn't. It was hopeless. The goodness of God was used as a hammer in my thoughts to condemn and demolish.

Why did I accept this? I was lied to and I accepted and repeated the lies of who I was and who God is. In my youth, I read the Bible rarely. I could quote some major verses. Reading it was a drudgery. Why did I go to seminary then? I was committed to following the direction of my life that I received when I was nine years old. I was going into music, period. And I wanted the music I did to be used to touch people for the Lord. This was part of the struggle in my life of wanting to be used by God but not having an intimate relationship with Him. But He never gave up on me. There were times of failure when it seemed that my dreams were crushed. The Lord lifted me up once again, and I followed one more little direction and made baby steps toward Him again. He just never quit. He never gave up on me even when I had given up on myself. He took everything, one by one, that could have destroyed me and made me just another statistic and worked it out for my good. I did have to stop fighting and arguing with Him so much. The more I let go of my way of destruction, the more I was led into the Way of life. None of this was because I was somehow more important or precious than others; it was all because of His love that is freely showered on us all. None of us deserve this. This is a free gift because He loves us.

Prayer

Lord, transform my eyes into Your eyes that I may see the truth. Transform my mind that I may think like You. Change my language that I may speak only what I hear You saying, just like Jesus did. Thank You that You want these things for me more than I do.

Verses 14–20

The Law is spiritual and I, in my flesh, am not. My old nature is subject to the power of sin. When I do what I really don't want to do but I do the things I detest, I am agreeing with the Law and hold it to be admirable. But I don't want to follow it in my flesh. The old sin nature is the one doing these things. Nothing good resides in my old fleshly nature. The power of sin rules in my lusts and appetites and I don't have the power to overcome it.

This is the condition of all of us. The new law of Christ is spiritual. My flesh is not. What was my old nature is not spiritual but it is dead. When I struggle between my new nature and the old, I am putting myself again under sin's influence. But I choose not to follow something that is dead.

I was a slave to that once and had no power over it. I was trapped and bound. If we are honest, we have all been in this turmoil. And as long as we are in these earth suits, we will have that pull of the flesh. However, it will diminish as we practice and exercise our faith. We are not condemned to defeat. We have been given a path to victory. We are right now overcomers because Christ has overcome, and we are in Him. He fulfilled and paid all the penalties for our Law-breaking. It's a done deal. If I still struggle, it's because I choose to remain under the old, dead influence. I can choose to agree with God that my old way of being is dead, and that I am now alive in Christ and live by a new directive, free of the debt that my sin deserved. This is the simplest and hardest thing to do. Turn from familiar death and choose new and unfamiliar life. It is so worth it. I wish I had done it sooner. Better late than never. Now I experience the acceleration in the kingdom that more than makes up for the time. Isn't God good! Isn't He wonderful!

Prayer

Help me, Lord! Let my awareness grow that the old nature is dead and should remain so. Open my eyes and heart to see my new life in You. Let me grow in greater intimacy with You to gain greater ground in Your kingdom. I want to explore and possess all that You have for me in this new life. The old is dead and rotten, and I want nothing to do with it. By Your Spirit and power, I stand in Christ and appropriate all that You have for me. I want nothing else.

Verses 21–25

My spirit longs to follow the way of God. My appetites want to control. There is this struggle between the spirit and the flesh—the new and old natures. God alone, through Jesus Christ, can deliver me from this struggle. I reckon myself dead, and I choose not to bring it up again.

I like how Graham Cooke describes the situation: "The old nature is dead but I am still dealing with some sin habits." I don't need to fret over them. They are temporary. The Holy Spirit will guide me into the truth about how I will be transformed and delivered from the old ways. That is really His concern and His job. I just need to agree with the plan. I don't need to buy into the lie that just because I have these habits means that my new nature doesn't exist. The enemy would like nothing better than to keep me in defeat. That's where I was for decades. I believed his opinion of me rather that God's. When I accept and believe what God says about me, then I get all the victory He has promised. He will not force overcoming on me when I still hold onto something dead. I must release the dead to cling to life. I'm going to cling to something. It might as well be truth and life. What did holding on to despair ever do for me anyway? There was no joy or victory. I chose to be miserable long enough. I don't want to do that anymore! I am no longer the authority over my life. I no longer give authority to the enemy. I follow the Authority who loves me and has the power to bring me through everything victorious. I choose life!

Prayer

Thank You that You have made all this possible. Thank You that the hard work has already been done by You. Now You want me to live and grow and expand in the Life You have provided for me. I am not dealing with these habits alone. You know the best way to transform me and I agree. I cooperate with You. I follow Your directions because they are life and joy and peace.

Discussion Opportunities

1. What kind of religious viewpoint were you raised under?

2. How much energy do you spend on doing things on your own?

3. What would it be like to be dead to the influences of negativity?

4. Which opinion of you matters?

ROMANS 8

Paul is back to addressing both Jews and Gentiles in this chapter.

Verses 1–4

Here's the final point: there is *no* condemnation or judgement for those who are embedded in Christ because His life-producing Spirit has set us free from the power and influence of sin and death. The Law could not do this because we were still slaves of our old natures. *But God* could do something about it and *did* by sending His Own expression of love, which came in the flesh to be the substitute and sacrifice for us who are destroyed by death. So the conditions of the Law are ended in us because we are no longer subject to the old nature. We are now fed and directed by the spirit of life.

My identity was such a mishmash. Intellectually, I knew that I acknowledged God the Father, Son, and Spirit. I accepted the scriptures as truth and His revelation to others down through the centuries. I affirmed that Jesus had come and died as the sacrifice for sin and had been raised to provide the way for relationship with God. These were the very strong thoughts in my head. In my heart, I was a mess. I was a wicked, evil, worthless thing who could not possibly be good enough for anything. I told myself this quite frequently. I would try to elevate my worth by doing "good" things or working hard for others. I had been born into a family of many pastors and teachers, so I was steeped in the Bible, its history and my own family's history in the church. For three generations, there had been preacher's and their wives in my lineage. I thought this would probably be what I would do. I was very active in my church and very devoted to the faith and everyone around me knew it.

In high school, people knew that I did not participate in the party and drug scene of the sixties. I heard the Beatles but rock music was not my favorite. And it was uncanny that three boys I dated during this time suddenly felt called to the ministry when with me. After we stopped dating, they pursued other things. Another boy even told me that he had to break up with me because I was too strong in my faith. It got to the point that I told God that whoever I dated needed to already have decided to be in the ministry before he met me. I wasn't going to fall for that ploy again. I ended an engagement because the guy was just trying to impress me and my mother and really had no desire to be a minister.

I went through college and into seminary pursuing what I felt was a call to music missions. I was involved in the Friday night street, witnessing teams. The team I was on went to the red-light district in Dallas. The women on the team talked to the working girls and the men talked to the johns. I was the prayer chairman for the team and felt very good about being involved in this. A fellow seminarian on the team started to talk to me, and we would ride together to Dallas and back. We discovered that we had gone to the same university. He was a Navy brat, and I was an Army brat. We had both moved a lot in our childhood. We were both the youngest in our families. We both felt called into full-time Christian ministry. It was really nice to have someone with so much in common and have a similar direction in life.

We began to date, and I so appreciated how he would listen to me and really converse with me. We would find churches, usually Catholic, that kept their doors open at night and go in and pray together. It wasn't until our fifth date that he even kissed me. I was impressed. I truly felt that this was someone I could be safe with and could trust. We dated for about six months, and he very nervously approached the subject of marriage. We talked about our own parent's marriages. He told me how he hated his father for how he treated his mother. I listened, kind of numb. I didn't recognize this as a warning signal. I had not yet started dealing with my own issues of childhood abuse, so my senses were totally offline. In my pride and arrogance, I thought that my love would overcome that hatred. My love would be powerful enough to make it all right. I certainly didn't know how to truly love someone because I despised myself. Train wreck waiting to happen...

I took him home to meet and talk with my mother and we became engaged. Years later, she told me that she wished she had never agreed to it. After we became engaged, things began to change. He revealed much more of his temper and rage. In my dysfunction, I began to assume responsibility for everything. It was always my fault. So often he would tell me that I *made* him do or say things. In my pride and arrogance, I thought I would be able to turn things around. I had no idea. I learned much later that if a person doesn't love themselves, it doesn't matter how much love is around them; they will not receive it. Rather than pay attention to these signs, I went ahead and married him. Things got much worse. Since he had conquered me, I was no longer something to spend any energy on. Now he refused to read the Bible and pray with me because he said, "I never saw my parents do it." Another time, he said he didn't like talking about scripture with me because I would get more out of it than him. Imagine, seminary students who can't read the Bible and pray together. About three months after the wedding, I became pregnant. I was so sick. He had no idea what to do with me.

The months went by and eventually, we had a delightful and beautiful baby girl. My mother and brother had been there for support which was much appreciated. After we all got home from the hospital and were settled, it was just me, my husband, and the new baby. Then, he left. Didn't say where he was going or how long he would be gone. For me, in my dysfunction, this was all my fault. I had no idea what I had done or what to do to make it better. Three days later, he came back and said that he left because the pressure of being a father was overwhelming to him. I can look back and see that this was the beginning of the downhill run. There was never an apology or reconciliation. This all fed and reinforced my belief that I was just wicked, evil, and worthless and deserved this treatment. I was imprisoned in these lies. I believed them. They were truth to me.

I remember reading the opening part of chapter eight and seeing "There is now no condemnation for those in Christ." I thought those were very nice words, but I was too deep in condemnation to even see or acknowledge that this freedom was a possibility. I was a drowning person trying to put on a very good show of living while dying inside. This was one of my arguments with God. I would read that there was no condemnation but would fight with God about just how awful I was. He couldn't possibly love anything like me. How dare He tell me of His love for me when I knew of His holiness and that He could not and would not associate with anything as wicked, evil, and worthless as me. Oh, God...I believed so many lies about myself and about Him. Yet, He never gave up on me.

We had another beautiful and delightful girl five years after the first and moved to South Texas. I got some excellent Christian counseling about eight years into the marriage. Two very intense years of daily work on the abuse issues from childhood. We moved again to Iowa, and things were not improving. The healthier I got mentally and emotionally, the worse the marriage got. I was no longer taking responsibility for his words or actions.

We went through two marriage counselors. I know I worked very hard to keep this marriage. One Sunday afternoon, he went down to the basement and brought back up a suitcase. He told me to pack and move out. At that moment, I literally felt a physical switch go off. "This is it. It's over. No need to try anymore." This was what went through my head. He had already told me two Christmas Day's in a row that he wanted a divorce. So a few months later, the girls and I moved out of the parsonage. It was the death of a dream and a relief at the same time. This was another step in my journey of growth and freedom. To be free physically like I was free spiritually took some adjustment. To become reliant on God's provision rather that a man's was a lesson in trusting. I have never been disappointed.

He had never failed me. The freedom and love that I have and know now has so far surpassed anything lost. God is so great!

Prayer

Yippee! Papa did it! My heavenly Father accomplished it all! There's nothing left to do but claim the victory over sin and death that Jesus bought. Walk and live it. You are my *hero*!

Verses 5–8

Those who choose to live by their old nature are led by it and that leads to destruction. Those who choose to live on the Spirit's level have a higher perspective and that leads to life and peace. The old is totally against God and His ways. It doesn't live by the law of love. It can't. Those who choose this are not following a path that leads to life.

The path I had been on lead to death and destruction, mine and others. As I went through those two very intense years of counseling to deal with the childhood abuse issues, I began to realize the profound effect I was having on my children. They were watching their mother be verbally and emotionally abused, and they were beginning to have it directed at them. Seeing this, I realized that there was no one else but me to stand in the gap to protect them. And there was no one but God to stand in the gap to protect and strengthen me. Choices became extremely important and significant. I no longer chose to take responsibility for someone else's words and actions. I had to realize I was not powerful enough to *make* anyone do anything, good or bad. This was certainly a blow to my pride but it was true. The healthier I got mentally and emotionally, the worse the marriage got because I was no longer agreeing with the dysfunction. I no longer chose the role of doormat.

Words coming out of my mouth astonished me and were seen by my children as very different than before. I was beginning to see the truth about who I was. I was choosing life. The old way was leading to death. The old way of thinking was full of lies about God and myself, and it led to destruction. My children were great motivators to see truth and be changed by it. At one point, my oldest daughter told me of a dream she had. This is what she related to me: "We were in Pizza Hut. The ceiling and the roof flew away. There was a helicopter above, and military men were descending into the restaurant. They began shooting at us, and you jumped in front of me and took a bullet. You died."

She was upset. I tried to comfort her and told her that in dream interpretation, when someone dies in a dream, it doesn't mean they die physically. It means they have been or are changing. They are not going to be what they have been. In the past, I had known about the truth, but it had never been applied to my life situations. By His grace and powerful presence, I began to change and learn by heart. By being around others who wanted this truth active in their lives, I saw and experienced it. There was an alternative to what I had chosen before. And there was the ability to choose it. God never gave up on trying to reveal truth to me and was relentlessly patient with me while I fought and struggled with it. Yes, the truth really can dawn on us. We really can come to our senses like the prodigal son and realize that we can make a better choice.

Prayer

Papa, You make it so simple. The enemy tried to convince me that I had no choices, that I was permanently stuck and trapped with no hope. *This is such a lie!* You are making me into the image and likeness of Christ and I have choices. This is one of the most liberating parts of Your good news. Choosing Your path and Your ways gets me off the path of death and on the delightful journey of life. I know the enemy hates this. His intention is to keep me as a slave.

Believing his lies befuddles me and takes away hope. I could even be duped into thinking that there is no alternative possible. *That's a lie!* Jesus paid the price so I could see that there is a choice and it brings life! Thank You! *Hallelujah!*

Verses 9–11

Don't live like people who don't love God. You live from a spiritual perspective since God's Spirit lives in you. If the Spirit of God is not in you, then you are not a follower of Christ. But since the Spirit does abide in you, then you are alive in your own spirit even though the body is no longer in control. In addition, since the Spirit of God who raised Jesus from the dead lives in you, then the God who raised Him raises you also from death into new life. This applies even in your mortal bodies because of the resident spirit in them.

This clearly speaks to who I am. This is a direct communication with no hidden meaning about how God sees me. Why did I fight this and not believe it for so long? As it says in 2 Corinthians 4:4, I was blinded by the enemy who worked to keep me in misery and darkness. And I agreed with it. *But God* didn't quit. He kept loving me and providing for me. Kept blessing me. Kept being faithful to me when I wasn't faithful to Him. Eventually, I was at a crossroad. The physical and emotional pain was so great, and I was having to spend extreme amounts of energy to keep it undercover. I came to the point where I could not continue as I had. This is what is known as hitting bottom in 12-step programs. The Lord lead me to 12-step programs to lead me right back to Himself.

Step 1: I *admitted we were powerless over alcohol (food, drugs, fear, controlling, etc.) and that our lives had become unmanageable.*

I had to admit first to myself that I couldn't do anything to get myself out of the mess I was in. Sounds hopeless. But then, Step 2, I *came to believe that a power greater than ourselves could restore us to sanity.*

Some people, some Christians, have a problem with this power greater than ourselves because it doesn't say God or Jesus. Some complain that a person could say that a turtle is a power greater than themself. But Step 2 qualifies the power by stating that it "restores us to sanity." There is no being or creature or substance that qualifies in these two areas except God. "Greater than ourselves" and "restores us to sanity" are pretty big requirements. We are allowed to take baby steps in this walk of faith and relationship. I was desperate and willing to try anything. That's exactly where I needed to be to let go and let God bring me back to Himself and sanity. I needed to stop arguing with God about how horrible I was and accept that He saw me as precious and delightful, wonderful and worthy. This changes your life when someone powerful and important believes in you. You start to see yourself through their eyes, and you think it could just possibly be true.

This relationship based on identification is not a new concept; it's just realizing that the Almighty God of the universe has wanted that close, intimate contact with me and has provided the way Himself for it to be. That is un-American. We're supposed to work hard and earn everything, pull-ourselves-up-by-our-own-boot-straps kind of people. This is such a lie. Nobody ever does anything totally by themselves. Everyone has had help along the way to accomplish anything. In Psalm 121, King David asks, "Where does my help come from? Help comes from the Lord." Pretty clear answer. Why did I fight all those years to do it alone and in my own strength? Saw where that got me, right? I want to live like who I really am. I don't want to spend so much energy in maintaining a facade that looks good on the outside but is full of putrid death on the inside. I want to be free to really live outside of cages and not be contained by walls. I want to be all that He says I am. And since His Spirit is in me, it can be done. He promised to lead me into all truth, and I hold Him to it. Don't really need to because His Word is His bond.

Prayer

Thank You, Lord, for having done this magnificent work! You thought of everything! I could have never accomplished this or even thought of it in the first place. If I were left to my own devices, I would try to perform and do good things with no power to achieve them. I would be hopeless. This is all possible because You have come to dwell in me. It is all possible because of You and Your plan.

Verses 12–13

So, friends, our old flesh-bound nature has no more legal right to control us. We are not obligated to live that way. If we choose that we choose death. *But* if we live choosing the life in the Spirit, we are dead to the flesh and no longer are possessed by lusts and appetites.

If is such a small word in the English language; yet, it is very powerful. It implies a proposition and possibly a promise. The smallness and simplicity of the word is such that a child can understand easily. *If* implies a choice. Since these verses reaffirm that we are no longer legally bound to destruction, then we can stand in the new life as new creations. We are not obligated or imprisoned by the consequences of our sin. *If* we choose life *then* we reap the benefits of life. This speaks to our freedom because if there is no choice, there is no freedom.

Jesus sacrificed Himself to open up the option for us to choose to live differently—more abundantly and vital. And when He ascended, He left the Spirit of God with us so we would have the power to make that better choice. In ourselves, we don't have the ability to make any difference in our lives. But with the Spirit, we have everything we need to choose this new life.

We are not on our own or left to figure it out by ourselves. We have a helper and a guide who knows us better than we know ourselves and who knows the way to get to our greatest good.

When I choose life in the Spirit, I am no longer trapped by my own knowledge and experience. We all have access to the greatest source of wisdom in the universe. Who wouldn't want that? Who am I to think that I know so much better? Why not avail myself of the life and power that God makes available to me? This is my choice. I've tried on my own and failed miserably. I argued out of my own pride to tell God that I was just fine, didn't need His help, and could do better anyway.

What a merciful and patient God He is. He never gave up on me but waited until I gave up my ranting so He could step in to rescue and heal me from all the wounds I had received from others and done to myself. I never loved myself until I accepted how much He loved me. His life-giving Spirit expanded in me as I let go of my feeble attempts at self-salvation. I am no longer entrapped by my pride and negativity. I am now encased in His grace which loves, protects, heals, and enjoys me being all I was meant to be.

Prayer

You have made a way where there was no way! Thank You, Papa! Thank You that, because You made me in Your image, I have the ability to choose life. And You gave me Your Spirit to give me the power to walk in that choice.

Hallelujah!

Verses 14–17

All who are directed by the Spirit are children of God. This is not a spirit of slavery taking you back into fear. This is the Spirit that makes us free children who can call on Papa. The Spirit of God joins with our spirits in testifying that we are His children and heirs. We inherit from God and are co-inheritors with Jesus. We shared His suffering. We share His glory.

I remember the Disney movie *The Prince and the Pauper*. It was a story of twins. One was raised in the palace as a prince and the other was out in the streets. Both were royalty but only one knew it. That was me. I had made a profession of faith and was baptized when I was seven years old. There had been several encounters through my adolescence and early adulthood, but I was feeling and acting like the pauper when all the time, I was really royalty.

The prince in the story had schooling from his infancy that taught him of his position in the kingdom. The pauper knew nothing about what he had been born into. I lived the exact same thing. There were smatterings and some encounters with God, but I was a pretty tough nut to crack. One of my incorrect premises was: "These are the commands I should live by, so how do *I* do that?" Wrong question. *I* did not have the strength or wisdom to follow the Lord at all. Jesus said it to his disciples, "Follow Me." They didn't have to think up or figure out what and when to do things that would qualify them as disciples. They were just supposed to follow. Jesus would lead. He would reveal and give insight. Then, when He ascended, He gave them (and us) the Spirit that would lead into all truth. What a relief! It wasn't up to me. I didn't, and couldn't, figure it all out or think it all up on my own. I could simply follow the Spirit and live as His much-loved child.

Accepting His love was a struggle initially because I spent so many years arguing with Him that I was unworthy of His love. I gave up. I stopped fighting. His love had conquered me. So I now agree rather than argue. I say yes instead of shaking my finger in His face. Now I let Him lead, and I follow because we both want me to be free and not a slave anymore. Now, when the Spirit tells me I am a royal ambassador of the kingdom, I say yes. Whatever You say I am, that's what I am. The Father identified me in Jesus's suffering, so I am also joined with Him in His victory. Who am I to argue?

Prayer

Papa, You do not want slaves or robots. You want relationships with Your children as free people able to be all You meant for us to be. This is the almost-too-good-to-be-true news that You want to and have already provided a way for me to be connected in fellowship with You. I couldn't have made it happen. Your Spirit joins my spirit. We are one, unified, with You. This is *glorious* and *amazing*!

Verses 18–26

Paul calculates that what we suffer now bears no comparison to the glory that will be. The universe itself eagerly waits for God's children to be revealed. The universe itself was kept from being what it could have been, not by its own choice but the choice of mankind who was given authority over it. *But* there was always hope. The universe will also be freed and experience the liberty and glory of the children of God. Even to the present, the universe groans in anticipation of its relief. We also groan waiting for the freedom the Spirit promises. Ours is a salvation full of hope. If we physically see it, then it is no longer hope. We live by faith, not by sight. By our hopeful patience, we show perseverance and endurance.

Hope is such a vital attribute of the Spirit of God in us. No hope equals despair and depression. Presence of hope means anticipation of fulfillment. There have been plenty of things in my past that I have hoped for and have seen come about. There are some things I still look forward to. With the negative and abusive things that happened in my life, I could have succumbed to hopelessness and misery. I certainly experienced those things, but throughout my life, God has not abandoned me or left me alone. He doesn't leave any of us alone. Even when we rale and argue, He doesn't turn and give up on us. He sees our future and knows that we will eventually stop the conflict and let love in.

The suffering we endure cannot compare to the glory ahead of us. I have lived long enough to look back and say, "It was worth it to be where I am today." And this awareness doesn't just affect us; it has an impact on everyone and everything around us. People and all creation are touched by our finally thinking, speaking, and acting like children of God. This is multiplied hope. This is exponential hope. This gives me the fortitude and stamina to endure and outlast the things that would seek to bog me down. This hope makes me buoyant so that I rise above and get the perspective of being seated in heavenly places with Christ.

Hope has an impact and does not come from me but is from the Spirit living in me. I don't have to stir this up myself. This is the heartbeat of God—knowing that victory is already won even in the middle of a battle. This is what all creation groans for—that the children of God realize who they are and act like it.

Prayer

I want Your Spirit of endurance, patience, and perseverance that bears me up through it all until Your liberty is perfected and complete in the whole universe. Thank You, Father, that I don't have to wait for this Spirit but that I can experience it now. Thank You that You gladly give me Your Spirit as a promise and a foretaste of what is to come.

Verses 27–30

In the same way that we experience hope, the Spirit comes to support and encourage us in our weaknesses. We don't even know how to pray. But even through our groans, the Spirit pleads for us and God, who knows us in our innermost being, knows what is meant. The Spirit earnestly intercedes for us in God's own language. In everything, we can be confident that His plan and purpose is for good for everyone He loves (and He loves everyone) and draws to Himself. God knew us before we existed here and so determined that we would be conformed to the likeness of Jesus. This way, Jesus would be the Older Brother in a family of children. This is how God sees us. These called ones are justified, gifted, and share in His glory.

Encouragement is so important. In Hebrews 3:13, we are told to encourage each other so that we are not made stubborn by the work of sin. I love this word. It comes from the French. I had a great-grandmother who came directly from southern France to America, so I always enjoyed pursuing the language. The French word for *heart* is *cour*. So when we speak of courage, we are talking about heartiness—strength of determination from our deepest being. To *encourage* means "to build up another's heart." We invest in each other's heart and strength when we encourage each other. This is what the Spirit does for us. There is the action of building up, growing, and maturing our innermost being by Him being the Greatest Cheerleader. But the Spirit is not just on the sideline cheering us on, He is inside us and with us always to help us and guide us in the best path.

With the Spirit of the Almighty God inside me helping me, why would I fight and think I somehow knew better than Him? Crazy, huh? Well, I gave up doing that and have had a much more positive and hope-filled life because of it. There are times, because of my human limitations, I don't even know what to ask God for. No worries! The Spirit in me understands even my wordless groans and can translate that for me into God's own language. How cool is that? I can know to the depth of my being that God only wants good for me and will work out everything, even hard times, to my benefit and for others also. I don't need to worry or fret. It is God's work to grow me into likeness with Christ, not mine. I just follow directions. I don't have to come up with a plan or an outline or a timetable. That's His job. My job is to follow and say yes, just like Jesus did.

Jesus is my Older Brother, and He has opened the way for me to follow and has put His Spirit in me to help me along the way. I can't lose in this situation. I only lose if I turn away from this relationship and think I can do this on my own. I have learned the hard way how bad it is to do this. My choices now are to daily follow the path ahead of me that He leads me on from glory to glory.

Prayer

Hallelujah! Your plan is *great!* It is not up to me. It is Your intention and determination that results in the conformity of Your children into the likeness of Jesus. I didn't plan it. I can't make it happen. All I do is agree to be drawn closer to You so that You can do this work in me. My efforts were death. Your way is life. I choose life.

I hope these chapters have been useful in revealing how beautifully God sees us. There are so many arguments and lies out in the world that work so hard to keep us down. What would really happen if the sons and daughters of God rose up in their complete identity and became true ambassadors of the kingdom? It would be world changing, atmosphere shifting. The universe itself groans waiting for this to happen.

These chapters have laid out a foundation. We build and grow on top of this solid rock. But wait! That's not all... The Bible has words that are specific and meaningful to each of us individually. I will share some of these in the following sections.

Discussion Opportunities

1. Where does condemnation come from?

2. What is the law of love as described in verses 5–8?

3. What does it look like to live by the Spirit?

4. What are you passionate about?

Part 2

JUST WHO IS GOD?

My premise is that I cannot know who I truly am without knowing who God is because my identity flows from Him. So here is just a smattering of truth about who God is. These are some of the names that describe God, His character and nature.

Adonai—Great and Mighty Lord	Deuteronomy 10:17
Elohim—All-Powerful Creator	Psalm 19:1
El Roi—The God who sees me	Genesis 16:13
El Shaddai—All-Sufficient One	Psalm 91:1
Immanuel—God who is with us	Matthew 1:23
Yahweh—I AM that I AM (Latin-Jehovah)	Exodus 3:13–14
Jehovah Rapha—I AM your Healer	Exodus 15:25–26
Jehovah Rohl—I AM your Shepherd	Psalm 23
Jehovah Nissi—I AM your Banner of Victory	Exodus 17:8–15
Jehovah Jireh—I AM your Provider	Genesis 22:12–14
Abba—Father	Galatians 4:6
El Elyon—God Most High	Psalm 7:17
Jehovah Shammah—I AM here	Ezekiel 48:35
Jehovah Shalom—I AM your Peace	Judges 6:24

If my mind is continually befuddled by lies about myself and God, I am wandering aimlessly in a fog. The truth is the only antidote for the darkness of lies.

In other places, I have described the background of my childhood. I came out of childhood into young adulthood with some pretty messed-up ideas about who God is. And as a result, I was filled with some "stinkin' thinkin'" about myself. I share my story so that others may relate to it. I want you to know that I understand the turmoil and pain you feel because I have felt it myself. However, the truth about the relentless loving nature of God has changed my whole perspective on myself and life in general. I had to get away from the picture and idea that God is some being off in the sky looking down, ready to zap me with one of His lightning bolts when I make a mistake. This was a real turnaround. God is not the source of negativity, judgementalism, or condemnation. God is love. God is freedom, grace, and mercy. If He didn't love us just as we are, warts and all, He would never have sent Jesus to pay the price for our freedom and open the way for a loving relationship with Him. And this was His idea, not ours. This was done by His initiative not ours.

God is good and only wants good for us. And I hear your question which used to be mine: "Why is there so much suffering, then?" God doesn't cause suffering. Jesus Himself told us:

In this world you will have suffering but celebrate because I have overcome the world (John 16:33).

The things others meant to use to harm us, God can take, turn around, and miraculously bring good out of it (Rom. 8:28). That's the good news! We certainly will have hard experiences but there is a Redeemer available and close by who can free us from the slavery of depression and woe. This is a good God who loves us and cares about everything in our lives. Nothing too big or too small. And this God wants a daily personal relationship with every one of us no matter what we have thought or done. Everyone! No one, whether they are extremely religious or a scoundrel, cannot do anything to make Him stop loving them. God doesn't have love. He is love.

Some would say this is a mushy, emotional blob. Nope, He is the powerful Lord who loves us no matter what and wants to work in and through us to bring us to the freedom and fulfillment He created us to have. We cannot change ourselves by ourselves. We need help. My willpower is not nearly strong enough. No one's is. This is a cooperative effort between us and a loving, trustworthy God who only wants good for us.

Whatever challenges come in our lives are not intended to harm or destroy us but to make us stronger, wiser, and closer to Him. God is closer than our hand or foot. Closer than our own breath. The exact moment that a person chooses to turn from the failures they have made in life and receive His love and grace, that is the start of a new life, do overs.

When anyone is united with Christ Jesus,
there is a new world. The old order has gone
and a new life has begun (2 Cor. 5:17).

Clean slates are great! I am not required to carry around the negative consequences of the mess I have made. Jesus can make me free. Free from lies. Free from burdens. Free from things I was never meant to bear. He is powerful enough to handle it all.

Cast all your cares on Him because
He cares for you (1 Pet. 5:17).

This is the truth and there's more… This is just a taste of how good God is for each of us. Get to know God for yourself. I had to. Don't just listen to me or preachers and teachers. Find out for yourself how good He is.

Anyone who comes to God must believe
He exists and that He rewards those
who seek Him (Heb. 11:6).

Yay! Rewards! You will be amazed when you seek Him with your whole heart. God is totally sold out for you and proved it when Jesus died demonstrating just how passionately He feels about us. This is what has changed my life. I could have become an embittered, lonely, depressed, angry old woman, drowning in the sorrows and failures of my life. *But God* had a different plan. He wanted my life to be full to overflowing with love and joy in spite of all that happened.

Those things are behind me now. I press on to the Glory before me so that I can attain true life in the gracious presence of my Savior.

Discussion Opportunities

1. Are you ready for a new view of God?

2. How has that angry God picture worked, anyway?

3. Have you discovered that God laughs (Ps. 2:4)?

4. Make a list of all the things God is for you.

INHERITANCE WORD
Psalm 27

I first encountered the term *inheritance word* when reading and studying the material written by Graham Cooke. *The Being with God*[1] series lead me deeper in my walk and awareness of personal intimacy with God. One of the tools I was introduced to was inheritance words which spoke to me not only of the context in which they were written but also of personal application for today. An inheritance word is a declaration of love and provision made *to me*. Since it is the job of the Spirit to guide us into all truth, this is one of the ways He does it.

The Spirit highlights some verse or chapter. Then, I meditate and think about and ask questions about it. I have a conversation with God and am made aware of answers and insights I had not seen before. This is always an activity of love—over and over again demonstrating His love. These are encouraging and instructional, directional and edifying words. I will share some passages that have been intensely used to grow my sense of identity in my life with God.

---

[1] All materials Graham Cooke has produced or written can be found at BrilliantBookHouse.com.

The Lord is my light and my salvation. I am not afraid. He is my Refuge. I dread nothing and no one. When others attempt to surround and defeat me, they are the ones who will stumble and fall. If an army comes against me, there will be no fear in my heart, and I will not be distracted from trusting God. I only ask one thing of God—I want to be with You all my life, to see Your beauty. He will keep me safe in hard times. He will hide me in the Secret Place out of the reach of distress. You raise my head high above the enemy, and I look down on them. I will praise Him in front of everyone and sing to Him. My deepest desire is to be with Him. You do not shun me or look at me with anger or disgust. You are my Savior and never reject me. My father and mother may reject me but You never will. Instruct me so that the greed of my enemies is destroyed. Make my path with You.

The liars and foes that come against me will be demolished. I shall see and do see Your goodness right now. Pay attention to the Lord. Be strong and courageous and patiently abide with Him.

I remember singing this passage in an old song of the church when I was studying voice at seminary. Great song. I had no personal relationship or understanding of it. It was not until a few years ago that I heard the phrase "Secret Place." This psalm was given as reference for it. Verse 5 specifically states, "He will keep me safe in hard times. He will hide me in the Secret Place out of the reach of distress." This hit me like a ton of bricks. You mean that I don't have to go through things alone? You mean that there is a refuge You have already prepared for me that can keep me safe? You mean that I can't earn or deserve this? This is available just because I am Your much-beloved child? I don't have to paste on a smile when I actually am crushed inside? I can run to You in hard times and be safe?

These were just some of the questions I asked God. Verse 5 kept being the answer. This verse became a banner flag over me when confronting difficult things. This was not a retreat from the fight but an elevation over it. If I would run to Papa, He would take me into the place where the enemy couldn't find me and lift me above so I could look down and see how small and weak my distresses are. Verse 6 tells me that He raises me high so that I can look down on them. He gives me a whole new perspective. He lets me see things from His point of view. This is *glorious*!

The people closest to me may turn from me (verse 10) but God never will. He will teach me and share His wisdom and insight with me so that those who come against me will fall and I will be safe. This spoke to so many lies that I had believed about who God is and who I am to Him. I didn't have to face any of the things I had endured alone. The effect of having faced things alone in the past were suddenly changed. The weight and burden that I assumed I had to bear from my childhood abuses vanished. Yes, they happened but the negative and destructive consequences were lifted off. The disastrous effect of dysfunction in the marriage just fell off. Yes, they happened but the heavy load of failure was gone. In my sixties, I am finally free. I go into the Secret Place daily to listen and discuss the guidance for the day. To me, praying involves a lot more listening that it used to. In the Secret Place, I can ask questions and I listen, expecting answers. Let me say here that I am not hearing voices. I get impressions. Thoughts come to mind. Pictures appear in my imagination. The longer I listen, the clearer the communication is.

Just like the Holy of Holies in the Jewish temple, the Secret Place only has room for one—one person and the glory of God. The Secret Place is within me and wherever I am. We can all go there one at a time to be with Him. This is a place carved out for freedom from distractions. It can be a physical place or an attitude of the mind. It can be when you are totally alone or around people. It is the most important place in my life because it is there I am most aware and focused on Him. He is always present, but sometimes I am so distracted that my attention and focus need to be redirected and attuned to His presence and His voice. There is no deadline or time designation to this. It can be in different locations during the day. I am in my Secret Place in my bedroom by myself. I can be in my Secret Place in the car running errands. I am in my Secret Place while I shop.

I am constantly in an attitude of listening and asking questions, praising, or thanking Him. There is no one right way to do this. The Father has multifaceted creativity, and I cannot box Him into anything. The Secret Place is for love and freedom. I receive encouragement and direction in this awareness. The Spirit can guide each one of us into the Secret Place that is best for us. Listen and let Him lead.

*****

The book and movie *The War Room* opened my eyes to the possibilities of the power available in the "Secret Place" prayer closet. Also, the small workbook by Graham Cooke, *Crafted Prayer*, (which is part of the *Being with God* series) taught me to listen more intentionally to what the Lord was saying. I learned to listen to the impressions that would come to my mind when praying for others. It was really a matter of agreeing with what was already being said by God.

We read in Hebrews 7:23–25 that Jesus intercedes for us before the Father. Romans 8:22–30 tells us that the Spirit understands even our wordless groans that we cannot verbalize and intercedes for us by speaking God's own language for us. So I listen to what Jesus and the Spirit are saying and agree with them. Then, I know I have what I ask for because I am agreeing with what they are saying. And they always agree with the Father.

I was taken on an interesting journey to practice and hone this skill. It all started with a dream… I had retired and had some time to do things. I thought of my mother's father who had been a pastor in Austin for many years. He had the habit of going to the area hospitals every day and praying for people whether he knew them or not. I could do that. I could go into the area hospitals and pray for people. So I called a hospital chaplain and told him what I was thinking of. He referred me to his boss over all the chaplains. I spoke with her and told her my desires. She said that HIPPA laws only allowed friends and family of patients in the rooms. Going into stranger's rooms would not be allowed. She told me of volunteer training and chaplaincy schools. I thanked her for the information. At church, I spoke to a retired nurse about my desire. She said that there was nothing to keep me from being in the elevators or waiting rooms or hallways. This encouraged me.

Sometime in the next week, I had that dream. I found myself in an old country store. The interesting thing about the place was that there weren't just front and back doors, but there were doors everywhere. I knew in the dream that this was my grandfather's store. On the counter in front of me were all the papers of ownership. Suddenly some young boys ran in and took all the documents. Before I woke, a voice said to me in the dream, "Don't let anyone steal your inheritance." I immediately awoke. This is what it meant to me: those who have gone before have blazed a path, and it is mine to possess. So I started with the hospital that was closest and went to the first floor and walked around and sometimes sat. I had a journal and pen with me. I rarely spoke to anyone and few spoke to me. I watched and listened. I saw what was happening around me with the people there. I began to write down what the Lord impressed me to pray. I prayed for patients and their families, all medical, clerical and administrative staff, lab techs, cafeteria workers, housekeeping and maintenance workers, and security guards.

Early in this experience, I went to a local hospital, and I was in the ER. There were no patients in the waiting room. About fifteen minutes had gone by, and a young female doctor came out to ask if I needed anything since they were not busy and could care for me right away. I told her I was fine and didn't need anything. We smiled and she went back in. Within five minutes, two very large security guards came out of their office and sat in front of me, cornering me in my seat. One black, one white. The man sitting closest to me began to question me about what I was doing there. I told him that I was there to pray for everyone—doctors, nurses, aides, techs, cafeteria, maintenance, housekeeping, security guards, patients, and their families. He asked what church I attended. I told him. I told him that I had spoken to the chaplain about doing this. After all this he said, "Well, my name is Cedrick. C-E-D-R-I-C-K. You can pray for me. And you can pray for my supervisor, Jim, back there, too." We laughed. Every time they saw me after that, it was always a smile and a wave. The Lord had me witness some very pressing needs—trauma, injury, sickness, and death. I would go to the hospital floors and the ER. I did that for about a year at one hospital and then went to another. I did the same thing after. And after another year, I went to a third hospital, same thing. Since I kept coming back, people began to recognize me and smile. Atmospheres were being shifted.

In the middle of the first year, I found out that the municipal court had open sessions, and anyone could go in the court room. I started going there and prayed as directed by God for the judge, clerk and bailiff, and the people who had offences against them and their families. I prayed that the Spirit would lead them to see how valuable they are to Him and their families and help them turn to Him to change their hearts and behaviors.

Very pleasant responses were received from the judge and bailiffs when they found out what I was doing there. One day after all the people on the docket had been seen and heard by the judge, she asked if I needed anything. I told her I didn't. She asked that I come up to the bench. I went and as I went, I quickly asked the Lord to give me the words to say to the judge. The judge asked if I were part of some community watchdog group that looked at local government bodies. I told her I was not. "Well, what are you doing here?" I told her that I was there to pray for her and the clerk and bailiffs, the offenders and their families. Her reply was, "Well, we certainly need prayer." After that, I was warmly greeted by everyone.

I also let my granddaughter's second grade teacher know that I was available to help her however she needed. She asked me to come on Thursdays to help fill the kids' take-home folders with the school announcements. I went every Thursday and filled the folders that every child would take home. I prayed for the child and the family that would be opening that folder. I prayed for the teachers and all staff at the school. I will only know in glory the events that happened in those homes.

Because of my musical background, I told the teacher that if she had any list of things she wanted the children to memorize and learn, I would be happy to set it to music so that they would remember it easily. She gave me the "water cycle," and I wrote a song for the kids, and they had a lot of fun and were very appreciative. It was delightful to be known by the classmates of my granddaughter and receive their affection.

There were many doors in my grandfather's "store," and each one is a gateway to more territory to be explored and possessed. This book is one of the doors that has opened to me. I am excited and anticipate great things as I gain admission to each one. This is what makes this life such an adventure. I know there are places and people in my life now and in the future that will be revealed at exactly the right time and place. I have been through enough to trust Him and follow His guidance. I have no fear but anticipation. No dread but joy. No worry but peace. He is with me; I am just fine.

The Lord told me that He wanted me to craft some prayers for my family members according to the guidance I received from *Crafted Prayers*. After I had distributed the prayers to them at Christmas, He had me start on my church family. Some of them I knew a little. Most only superficially. But the Lord had things that he was praying for them, and I wrote them down and gave them these prayers. I listen because He never stops speaking and is always brilliant and sometimes hilarious. The Secret Place is where I live. I never leave it. I take it with me wherever I go. And there's always room for more. There's a Secret Place waiting for you.

Discussion Opportunities

1. How does this impact your understanding of what God has for you?

2. Think about the Secret Place in relation to His provision for you.

3. Open yourself to the adjustment of being raised above your enemies. What does that do?

4. Meditate on "But as for you." What changes do you imagine will come that are different than what is around you?

INHERITANCE WORD
2 Corinthians 1:19–22

*J*esus, the Son of God, is never a blend of yes and no. He is always a *yes for all the promises of God. This is why we glorify Him and say amen. We belong to Christ and are guaranteed and anointed by God. This is His work in us. He has set His seal on us as a promise of what is to come. He has given us the Spirit to live in us as the guarantee of that promise.*

This harkens back to Song of Solomon 8:6:

> *Wear me as a seal upon your heart, as a seal*
> *upon your arm; for love is as strong as death.*

These verses so clearly tell me who He is and who I am.

Concerning God's promises, Jesus is always a yes to them all. His Promises are true and sure. God's promises never expire. If He bound Himself to a covenant centuries ago, it still stands. His Word is not conditional or situational. His promises are based on His faithfulness, not ours. And since I (we) belong to God, it is guaranteed, and I carry the assurance of His presence and blessing. This is the work He does from the inside out. We are sealed to this fulfillment of what is to come. We are not only sealed into this covenant, but everything else is sealed out. This is something I must be aware of. Since I am sealed and encased in this promise, I cannot agree with and let people or things into my life that are harmful. I should not choose to play with or dally with things that will only bring me down. This does not mean that I cloister myself away from the world. It means I walk out in the world being an influence on them like Jesus rather than them influencing me. I am an ambassador for the kingdom. A good ambassador does not double-cross the kingdom that sent him. I am to be faithful because my King, who lives inside me, is faithful. This is a deeply personal and intimate relationship. This is more than just wearing a ring on the finger or having a passport. I failed at this for so many years.

I tried to keep up the outer appearance, but my heart was still going after my own way. I tried to solve problems in my own intellect. I looked for love and acceptance because I had not let in the love of God that was already there. My pride thought that I could figure it out by myself, and I was deluded into thinking that I was supposed to anyway. I was believing so many lies. I had to come to the end of myself and all *my* wisdom to realize I didn't know anything. This was when the Lord stepped in and impressed me with, "Are you done? Want to try it My Way now?" I surrendered. There was no fight left. Then, He began to teach me who I really am and who He really is. I look back on those decades of struggle and ask why. I had based my attitudes on lies and had been so stubborn and fearful that I fought against the One who loved me no matter what and never abandoned me. This One who is faithful and true never expected me to figure things out without His guidance. He is in charge now. I listen. I follow. He teaches. I learn. He downloads His wisdom and I praise Him. He opens my viewpoint to His perspective, and I understand like I have never understood before. This is only the surface of what He has promised. There is so much more to come. His Spirit guarantees it.

This picture came to my imagination concerning the seal set on my heart.

Discussion Opportunities

1. How will it change your viewpoint if you know that Jesus is always a yes to all God's promises?

2. How does it change your attitude to know that the Spirit is the promise or guarantee of things to come?

3. Does this give you more confidence and assurance of His faithfulness?

4. What thoughts or attitudes are having to change?

INHERITANCE WORD
Isaiah 30:23–26, 29–30, 32

Y ou, Melody, will no longer weep or be depressed. I, the Lord, demonstrate favor toward you and answer your every call for help. You, Melody, have certainly endured a time of adversity and affliction but I who teach you will be revealed. You will always see Me with your own eyes.

If you stray to the left or right, you will hear Me with your own ears. My voice will direct you in the best path. Everything false will be completely removed from you.

Your efforts at "seed planting" will be blessed and nurtured until there is an abundant harvest. The resources I give you will themselves be blessed and multiply.

Each level of higher ground will have its own source of refreshment. Disbelief will fall.

Radiance greater than sun or moon will be released when broken limbs and wounds are healed.

There may be calamity around, BUT AS FOR YOU there will be festival songs. You will have a glad and joyful heart just like when entering My presence. I am your Rock and Strong Tower.

You will hear My voice in majesty and power. These will be seen in My passionate fire.

All kinds of percussion instruments will beat in time with My rhythm.

Hindsight is 20/20

From my childhood, I knew God was there. I knew a lot about Jesus. I knew some about the Father but hardly anything about the Spirit. I knew God was there, but I was always wanting a deeper connection, and there were so many lies and things that got in the way of that relationship. The enemy took what had happened in my life and used it to make some very convincing distractions. But I knew that He was there from the beginning, and that was confirmed the older I got.

To begin, my legal name is not Melody. On my birth certificate it is Mary Lilane. My mother named me Mary after her friend. Mary was an RN at the VA hospital. She had studied voice at Julliard and had an MA in American lit. My mother was the one who led her to Jesus. Years later, she also taught at Christ for the Nations. When I was just a week old, mother said that she awoke and heard Mary taking care of me and singing to me. It was a song based on Isaiah 30:29:

> *But as for you, there shall be songs as on the night*
> *of a sacred festival. You will be glad just like*
> *those who march to the sound of the flute on their*
> *way to the Lord's temple, the Rock of Israel.*

Mother heard Mary say to me, "You're just a little song in the night. I think I'll call you Melody." From a few weeks old until now, that is how I am known. Very few people know me by my legal name. Doctors and official papers must have my name as shown on my birth certificate. But Melody has been the name that my family and friends know me by.

My middle name Lilane was made up by mother. She was named *Lillian* after her father's mother, and she wanted to continue the name so she made up *Lilane*. I carried it another generation further by giving my youngest daughter the middle name *Suzanne* which is French for *lily*. I have felt for a long time that this was how God got me called the name He wanted me to have.

This is not a unique event. There are many records in scripture when God named people or changed their names. Abram became Abraham, Sarai became Sarah, Jacob became Israel. God's name for Solomon was Jedidiah because He loved him and chose him. Jesus changed Simon's name to Peter and Saul became Paul. The angel announced to Elizabeth and Zachariah that they would have a son and told them to name him John. Joseph and Mary were told that the Son of God would be named Jesus. God knows these things, and it all matters to Him. This is part of our identity. How am I known to God? What does He call me? Naming something doesn't just denote authority over it. It evokes responsibility and love for the one being named. This cherished one that is special and unique has a wonderful name, and the Lord delights in calling us by name. That's just another example of how close He is and how much He cares. In her distress over not finding the body of Jesus, it was when Jesus said her name, Mary, in just the way that only He did that she finally recognized that it was Him. I pray that you will experience this level of identity and intimacy with the One who knows you best and loves you most.

In the late seventies, Bill Gothard Seminars were pretty popular. While I was in Ft. Worth, Texas, at seminary, he came to Dallas. On one session, he spoke about music, and my ears pricked up. Then on a large screen, there appeared:

MELODY—Raises our spirits to God
HARMONY—Teaches fellowship in diversity
RHYTHM—Lets us hear the Heartbeat of God

There in bold print was my purpose. I was born to help raise people's spirits to God. That was a commissioning experience for me. I went back to school with a renewed direction for study and development.

A couple of years ago, when reading about inheritance words, I started to look at the verses before and after verse 29 and realized there were promises, provisions, and protections for me. The prophet Isaiah may have been saying these words to Israel, but the Spirit was directing them right at me. I inserted my name and received all of this as mine personally. Verse 23 says I no longer need to weep or be depressed. That is over and done. The Lord was manifesting favor over me and promised to answer every call for help. The Lord confirmed that I had endured a time of adversity and affliction, but He was going to reveal Himself to me. He promised I would be able to see Him with my own eyes. (Today I see Him in my spirit; one day it will be face to face.) If I happen to get distracted or get off course, He will redirect me, and I will be able to hear and understand. I will know His voice and will follow it. (Love this!)

Everything false, negative, and destructive will be removed from me. My efforts at spreading the good news will be blessed and developed until there is an abundant harvest. The resources He gives will, themselves, be multiplied. Each new level of development will have its own source and provision of refreshment. Disbelief will fall away because belief will become so strong, it will push the unbelief out since there simply will be no room for it. Brightness greater that the sun will be released when broken limbs and wounds are healed. (Yes!) There may be disturbances around, *but as for me*, there will be songs. My heart will be glad and joyful just like when I enter His presence. He is my Rock and Strong Tower. I will hear His powerful voice and His majesty will be seen in His passionate fire. All kinds of rhythm instruments will play in sync with His heartbeat.

Yes, I took this for myself. But God is big enough for you to claim it also, plus much more. This is done by listening to the Spirit and letting Him highlight His Word to you for personal application.

Discussion Opportunities

1. Are you aware of confidence rising up?

2. Are you starting to see how these promises can apply to you?

3. How does personally applying scripture effect your relationship with God?

4. If you haven't done it yet, put your name into John 3:16 and realize how personal that makes it.

   For God so loved _____ that He gave His Only Son that if _____ believed on Him _____ should not perish but have ever lasting life.

INHERITANCE WORD
Isaiah 55:1–5

Come, who are thirsty, get water.

Come, who are hungry, buy corn and eat. Can't buy with money, but there is a price.

Why spend your money for what is not bread and spend your labors on what doesn't satisfy?

Listen to Me and you will have good nourishment and enjoy the best of the land.

Come, listen, hear My Words. Then, you will have Life.

I will make a promise that is eternal to love faithfully as I loved King David. He was My Witness to the world, a prince to the nations. You, in turn, will bring nations you do not know. They shall come running to you because the Holy One has glorified you.

After all the searching and looking in all the wrong places, this passage gives the most satisfying answers. Come, if you're thirsty and hungry. Here is the source to remedy the deepest needs. It can't be bought with money. Why pay so much for what doesn't fulfill?

"*Listen*...pay attention and you will be fed, and your thirst will be sated. You will enjoy the provision from Me. Come, listen and you will know and experience true life. This is a forever arrangement. I love you faithfully and passionately. Look at the others I have loved, and let them bear witness. These testify about Me to the nations as to how well I love. You will call to nations you don't know. These nations who don't know you will come running because they see that you honor and love Me. I will exalt you because you have chosen to find your life in Me."

This is a personal word of relationship with the Father. All the years of floundering around and looking to people and things and substances are over. I have found the source of satisfaction for my soul. There is no one and nothing that can do this. I know what it is to look to people. The problem with humans is that they are just so darn human! They are no greater a resource that I am. They have the same feet of clay that I do. I had to stop looking to people to fill my deepest needs. Achievements and degrees did not fill the bill either. Goals were met but there was no fulfillment in my soul. They were intellectual but none addressed the wounds or needs of my heart. Substances didn't work either. Over-indulgence made things worse in fact. They only added to the guilt and shame.

Look at the question in verse two: Why do you give the price of your labor and go unsatisfied? The advertisers tell us that if we buy their stuff, we will be happy. What a crock! It's a lie. Nothing physical on this earth will meet the needs we have for love and emotional healing. The invisible things of the Spirit are the only things that satisfy the invisible parts of us. This turns my focus from working so hard for material things that do not last or fulfill to pursue those things that really matter and make for true joy. Because I am a spiritual and eternal being, I want what lasts and can never fade or be taken away. This is His eternal promise to all of us.

Discussion Opportunities

1. What are you hungry and thirsty for?

2. Are you ready to stop looking to people and things to give you what only God can?

3. Romans 12:2 tells us to be "transformed by the renewing of our minds." How does this passage change your mind?

4. All this satisfying provision that God has for us is available because He loves us so much. Are you open to this great love?

INHERITANCE WORD
Psalm 91

Y ou, *Melody, live in the shelter of the Most High and dwell under the shadow of the Almighty. You say, "The Lord is my safe retreat. My God is the security in which I trust. God Himself will snatch me away from traps and raging tempests." Melody, He will cover you with His strong hands and cover you with His wings. You will not fear the predator's trap at night nor the arrow that flies by day, the disease that stalks in the darkness nor the plague that rages in the middle of the day.*

A thousand may fall at your side or ten thousand close at hand, but you, Melody, they shall not touch. His truth will be your shield and protective wall. With your own eyes, Melody, you will see this and watch what happens to those who try to hurt you.

For you, Melody, the Lord is a safe retreat. You have made the Most High your refuge. No disaster shall hurt you. No calamity shall destroy your home. He has assigned His messengers to guard you wherever you go. They will lift you on their hands to protect you. You will encounter dangerous things, but you will be safe.

Because you love Me, Melody, I will deliver you. I will lift you beyond danger because you know My name. When you call, I will answer.

I will help in times of trouble. I will rescue and lift you to honor. I will satisfy you with long life so that you can fully enjoy My salvation.

This psalm tells me how cherished I am. It speaks of being rescued and hidden away from all that would seek to harm me. This was my heart's cry for so long. I screamed for it, but I believed the lie that I was alone and there was no one to help or save me. Externally, I could look and sound fine, but internally, I was a wreck. What changed? Awareness. Revelation. Understanding. The Spirit never stopped working to convince me of His love and my value to Him. Even when I was yelling inside to be helped, I was concurrently pushing Him away because I believed that He could not possibly want to save me. I was weak and damaged and a failure. His love and power were not for me. They were for others more worthy. Yet, He still kept working at the little chinks in the walls I had erected. I cannot give a definite year or day when I realized that my perspective was completely changed. I know it was gradual, complete, and thorough. Now I claim these verses for myself. Now they are promises for me. Now I find myself safely beneath His wings. I stopped rejecting His passionate love and came in from the blizzard of despair. Now I have a confidence in His promises for me. Now the arrows, plagues and pestilences do not cause me to run in fear. I am hidden safe, and those things do not scare me anymore. I am shielded by His presence, and anything that tries to come against me only makes me burrow into Him even closer.

I do not fight these things alone or in my own strength. Thousands fall at my right hand. I am no longer an easy target. I have come into the fortress of His love and now experience emotional and mental safety and protection like never before. Fiery darts still come but they don't get through to injure me. I see them coming, and they don't penetrate His shield of grace around me. He is my retreat and refuge. His has even assigned ministering spirits (angels) to guard me. I have an entourage. He is more concerned about me than I am.

Verses 14–16 are from the Lord's perspective about how He redeems those who love Him. These are promises that never expire.

"When you call, I will answer. I will be with you, raise you up and bring you to a position of honor."

I took karate during my last year of college. The teacher was a black belt of many degrees. There were about thirty-five in the class—men and women. We were in our uniforms learning the moves. Every class, the instructor would tell each one where to stand. There were about four rows of us in a large long room with mirrors. As the semester went on, I realized that every time he put people in different places, I was put in different rows and positions. I saw that the students who were on the front row were the more enthusiastic and better learners. And just because you were in the front row one time did not guarantee that you would be there the next class. This was motivation to me. I worked hard in class and practiced often in my dorm room. I remember the first time the instructor called my name and placed me in the front row. I was shocked. He had told us previously that he put people in the front row so they could be a model for those behind them of how to do the moves correctly. This made me want to be even better.

"I will raise him to honor" (verse 15) is a picture of God recognizing the passionate heart of love in us. This can be everyone's experience. When I abandon myself to Him, I am drawn closer. This is His promise for us all. "I will satisfy with long life and give the fullness of enjoyment in redemption." (Verse 16).

I can look back on these events and see that even then He was demonstrating His love and care for me. He was teaching me practically about how He views me and wants to elevate me out of my messes and put me safe in Him. He wants me to be an example to others about how He saves and raises up those who will let go of all the lies about Him and themselves. He wants others to see how well we are so they will want to be well also. Accept the invitation.

Discussion Opportunities

1. Can you claim this as a promise for yourself?

2. What lies are still fighting for you attention in your head?

3. Are you willing to start believing God about Himself and yourself?

4. Are the misconceptions you carry really that important?

INHERITANCE WORDS
John 8:12, 31–32; 17:22–23

My favorite Inheritance Words are the ones that are straight from Jesus. The Gospel of John is the most personal of the eye-witness accounts of Jesus's life and teachings. These words speak most directly to me and how God sees me and how I should see myself. Repeatedly, Jesus states who He is and that we are just like Him. He identified completely with us so that we could identify with Him.

> *I AM the Light of the world. No follower of Mine will wander in darkness. They shall have the Light of Life (John 8:12).*

I don't have to go through life confused and in despair. Followers of Jesus will not wander in the dark. There will be light around and in them. If I find myself in confusion, then I get much closer to Jesus by reading His teachings and listening better to His guidance. Anyone who lives in His light will have light in their life. This is a process but one with hope and purpose. When I seek Him, I will find Him, promise.

If you abide in My Revelation then you
are indeed My Followers. Because of this
you will know and experience the Truth
and be set free by it (John 8:31–32).

What a promise! Abiding in Him will lead me into truth about God, myself, others, and the world. I will be set free of all the burdens and negativity in my life. That is exciting! Freedom comes because I see things from the perspective of God.

The Glory that You gave Me, Father, I have given
to them so that they may be unified as We are One.
I AM in them and You are in Me so they can be
perfectly, completely whole. Because of this unity
the world will learn that You sent Me and You
loved them just like You love Me (John 17:22–23).

God's favorite number is one. The desire of His heart is that there be unity and oneness between us and God. This does not mean robots cut out of cookie cutter molds. His creativity is too diverse for that. Every individual is appreciated for their uniqueness. His plan is for there to be love, acceptance, and the very best, most wonderful life for each of us. There is no tolerance of destruction and negativity. Any attitude or thing that degrades, abuses, or demeans us is simply not part of His way.

These verses were part of Jesus's last prayer before the crucifixion. It was that important. Oneness is His priority. Without this identity in Him, I only see myself as an orphaned pauper. Seeing myself as He views me, as a valuable part of the kingdom, I can be all I was created to be. Being closely joined to God did not happen because I worked for it or earned it; my position in Christ is because the Father has placed me in Jesus. Jesus paid the price for this to happen. I couldn't do this through my own efforts. It's been done for me. Yahoo! So that's who I am—a much-loved child of God. He didn't want heaven without me, so Jesus came to make the way possible. He has taken something wallowing in the mud and lifted it up, cleaned it off, and gave a new identity—oneness with and in Him. That's the good news. That's what I base my life on. That's all there is, and that's all I need.

Discussion Opportunities

1. How is your view of God changing?

2. How is your view of yourself changing?

3. What effect will this have on your daily life?

4. Practice saying yes to the Spirit's impressions. How different is this to what you usually do?

Part 3

FATHER RELATIONSHIP

The Fatherliness of God has been an extremely important part of my relationship with my Heavenly Father. Even before I knew the full extent of His abiding presence and power and his desire for an intimate relationship with me, He was still breaking through, little by little, my cages and prison walls.

When I was a junior in college, I attended a smaller, more residential church in the community. It was not one of the mega-churches in town that most students attended. The pastor was doing a sermon series on the fruit of the Spirit (Gal. 5:22–23). His Sunday morning sermon had been on love. I went back Sunday night, and the topic was joy. I was by myself sitting on the aisle. Across from me were two sweet old ladies. I began to cry. Internally I was yelling at God. "I don't know this joy… What on earth is it like? Why can't I experience it?" The ladies just looked across the aisle at me crying while the preacher talked about joy.

After the service, I spoke to the pastor's wife for a little while. She recommended that I go to the counseling center on campus since it was free. I did. At my appointment, I sat down with the counselor. He started by asking me about my parents and family. I was twenty at the time, and I told him of my father's death when I was twelve. He was excellent at asking the right questions and was really listening

97

to my responses. Eventually he said, "You know, I don't think you've ever let the wound from your father's death heal." It was incredible. He had put his finger on exactly what was true. I felt a huge weight lift off me with this understanding.

I went back to my pastor's wife and told her all that had happened. She said, "Well, you know there's something you can do about this, right?" I asked what that might be. She knew that I had made a profession of faith in Jesus as a child, but she suggested that I could also accept God as my personal Father. This blew my mind. No one had ever told me anything like this before.

We continued to talk about what kind of father the heavenly Father is. He's never tired or sleepy. Never has to leave to go to work. Never has a headache or is sick. Never runs out of provisions and resources. Always loves. Always is patient and understanding. Loves all His children uniquely. Always forgives and restores. Is always delighted with us. Never dies. Is always present. After going over all these attributes, I accepted God as my personal Father. That was a major healing and another example of how He doesn't quit or give up on loving us. These forty plus years since that time have only become sweeter, more intimate, and meaningful for me. I know that He is my Father, and I am His beloved child…no matter what.

I must add the most current revelation I've received. Because of the experience of pain related to my father's death, I pretty much turned away from him. I fully embraced God as my Father. This was good but recently my pastor, Richard Neusch, spoke of the wells Abraham had dug, and that Isaac set about to reopen and benefit from the work of his father. This was an act of honoring the work of the one who went before. Isaac received blessing because he honored in this way.

I don't believe in coincidence. I believe God has a plan and purpose and can make anything work toward my good. Several months ago, a cousin of mine went to a funeral in the Houston area. He related to me that a woman there had mistakenly identified him as his father, the twin brother of my mother. He corrected her and said that the one she remembered was his father. She went on to say that she still remembers my mother, Lillian, and my father, John, when he pastored at Manchester Baptist Church. She related how much my parents were loved and how much my father's ministry meant to her and others. My cousin thought I would like to hear this. It was a real treat out of the blue.

My father went into the chaplaincy in the army from that church in 1944. He was a career chaplain who was in Japan (before I was born), Germany, and Korea (two tours). His was a life of serving. It just did not end well because of overwhelming forces that were never dealt with. He tried to carry it all by himself.

When I listened to Richard's sermon about honoring those who had gone before, I was truly convicted. I had not honored my father. I had turned from him. As God had arranged, I was scheduled for my annual Sozo the following day. It was in this setting that the picture of my well and its significance was revealed. I was in my mind the well that my father had dug by hand. It did not have the brick wall around it with a little roof and a bucket to pull up and down. It was just a hole in the ground. It had a long wooden pole going deep down and extending high out of the hole. The area around the pole was all filled in with dirt and rocks. I asked the Lord how the dirt and rocks could be removed. He replied, "I could blow them out." I asked Him to do that. I asked what the wooden pole was for, and He said that it was there to keep it from caving in, thereby losing access to the water.

This was a most amazing picture and interpretation. Access was regained to the cool, fresh water. I pour this water over myself, my children, and grandchildren and we are blessed.

This has changed me. I have turned back to my father and all that he did in faithfully serving God and the country. I asked for forgiveness for having turned my back on him and have received blessings from this work laid out by my father. I was further directed by the Lord, "Honor My servant, John." This is what I do now because in honoring my father, I am also honoring God. Now I wash myself and my whole family in the water of His Word. I say, "Yes, Lord."

I will not reject any provision the Lord has for me. Thank You that You orchestrated everything to bring honor and glory to Himself and help me walk in truth and revelation. This is the precious walk that is available to all of us. Trust Him. He is trustworthy.

Discussion Opportunities

1. Ask the Father how He sees you. Write your response.

2. How do you see the Father?

3. Is there someone or something you have rejected that the Lord might open your eyes to see greater blessings?

4. Ask the Lord to show you how this can be done.

The answers can open up awareness of things that might need the Spirit's help to work on.

IDENTITY AWARENESS

I n ancient times, the people of God were called the Hebrews. In the Hebrew language, *Hebrew* is "Ivri," singular for an individual. *Ivrim* is plural for the nation. The root word for *Ivri* is *avar* which means "to cross over." The *Ivrim* are people who "crossed over." In order to leave the land of slavery, they had to cross the Red Sea. To enter the Promised Land, they had to cross the Jordan River. They were people who were known for crossing over. They left one place for another. It was the ending of one life and the beginning of another. As a follower of Messiah, I am a spiritual Hebrew. I am a person who crosses over, passes through a barrier, breaks through a wall. I must leave one place and enter another. The *Ivrim* were people who had known two realms. The one who is "born again" has crossed over—left the old for the new. Darkness to light. Jesus was called the King of the Hebrews (*Ivrim*). He crossed over the ultimate barrier from death to life. He is the Ultimate *Ivri*. He has the power to overcome any obstacle.[2]

I am an *Ivri* because I have crossed over. I have gone from lies to truth, destruction to restoration, degradation to exaltation. This has been and still is done by the power of the King of the *Ivrim* in

---

[2] Hebrew terms and translations from *The Book of Mysteries* by Jonathon Cahn.

my life. I am not hopeless but hopeful. Jesus so completely identified with my condition and took it all on Himself so that I could be completely identified with Him. Everything that had come in my life with the intent of destruction was changed into numerous stepping-stones from one level to another, one upgrade to the next, glory to glory. This is in my DNA. I am a "crossover" person. I have left a place and have entered a new one. I do not drag the baggage of the old into the new because the old doesn't work anymore in the new. It served its purpose but it's done now. For instance, the manna that the Israelites had eaten for forty years in the wilderness stopped when they entered the Promised Land. There was milk and honey, grapevines, and ripe fields of grain to sustain them. The old was of no further need. Children only need a liquid diet for a short time. When they develop to a certain point, they must begin with soft foods. Eventually they go to more solid foods. If they stayed on the milk, they would not grow and thrive.

For so long, I was feeding on the food of slavery, not growing, not thriving, in fact, dying. No more! I am a new creation and I know it! I consume the food of the Redeemed! Food from the King's banquet. I have crossed over into life and growth, favor, and grace. My eternal life has already begun. When I do my next crossover into glory, that life will continue forever. There is an invitation to crossover and experience the benefits of being alive in Christ. Respond. None of us does this by our own power or smarts. It is done in the realization that we can't do this for ourselves. The Israelites could not have caused waters to build up like a wall or a wind to blow all night so the river bed was dry. There was One who provided the way for them because of the great love He had for them. This is what is done for us today. We cannot engineer our own rescue. Why would we when the way is already available? Take hold of the King of crossovers, and He will get you safely through. How has trying all this on your own worked for you, anyway? Let go of the stuff that only enslaves you, and hold on tight to the One who cares more about your freedom than you do. Come on, let's crossover!

PROPHECIES

Current prophetic words also speak into my identity. This is an additional exercise in listening. It was January of 2018 that I felt impressed to start writing this book. I had already written and shared the passages from Romans 5–8 with about ten women, sending it to them as a daily devotional. The Lord led me to start with what He had already given me. As encouragement, there were words spoken over me that I received as direction and confirmation from God.

Every year at my church, True Life Fellowship, we have a women's conference. This year in March 2018, we had three women speakers. Rene Evans was the first presenter of the weekend, and she opened us up to welcoming the wild-goose chase that the Spirit can take us on. He loves to take us on adventures. At the end of her sermon, she prophesied, "I feel like there is someone in the room who is in the middle of writing a book. And you keep asking the question, 'Who is going to read this?' The Lord says, 'This is an adventure I'm pulling you into,' and He is with you." There were about two hundred ladies there of all ages from all over central Texas, and this was pointed right at me. I went up to Rene at a break and introduced myself and told her that the prophecy was for me because I had started writing a book. Talk about confirmation!

Also, in January 2018, Lana Vawser, a prophet from Australia, posted on January 13: "What you write is about to take flight." She went on to say that "breakthrough and birthing was upon writers. They would write with greater ease, clarity, insight, and flow. The words being written are coming with fire anointing, grace, and great impartation. These writers are breaking new ground in spite of the opposition. They are being given road maps and blueprints for others to follow. A prophetic mantle and anointing are upon what many are writing for the Lord in this season whether recognized or not. Be *intentional* in stewarding the assignment God has given you. You will see a mighty move of the Spirit of God upon this writing. Great favor will fall upon your stewardship of this assignment He has given you. He will take His words through you further than you imagined." Then Lana referenced Isaiah 30:8 in the message and New Living Translation. This was also from Isaiah 30, which is a chapter of my inheritances. How cool is that (see chapter 7)!

February 1, 2018. Lana Vawser prophesied again concerning writers: "Many prophets are called to write more and in different ways in this season. The writing of the Lord will be dripping in such revelation, anointing, and impartation for encounters that there will be a great harvest from your writing. There will be great acceleration on the writing in this season. No more delay but fruitfulness and increase upon your words."

This was further encouragement that I needed to have to see me through to the end of this task. Then again, on May 13, 2018, Vawser prophesied that Scribe Angels were being sent with assignments for women to write. "A significant increase of the *scribe anointing* is being released. As they spend time with the Lord, the writings are *drenched* in a *breaker anointing* to unlock and free."

This is identity and calling, designation, and motivation. This whole process of putting everything that He wants included in this book has been a work of releasing and unbinding what He wants to be freed. This is my identity—to raise people to God. It is accomplished in following His directions. That's always the best way.

How wonderful and precious is God to direct me in January 2018 to start this and then give me words of confirmation. You don't ignore things like that! This is the adventure I'm on right now. When this part is finished, I have no idea what will follow, but I know it will be an adventure. I will grow closer to Him, and I will be stretched and exercised to greater strength for the kingdom…because, you see, He wants me to fly! He has had me in the process for many years of divesting me of baggage that was only holding me down. He wants me free! He wants my hands empty so that He can fill them with the riches of glory. Join me! Let's soar! Let's be wild geese!

*****

I worked through the prophetic course offered by Graham Cooke. The three books were very in-depth. Not something to go through quickly. At the conclusion of each book was a prophetic word from Cooke about what would be happening in the lives of those who had studied. I found so many personal applications in what was foretold.

To begin, the word at the end of the first book, *Approaching the Heart of Prophecy*, stated that I will "become highly confident" in God, and that He has given "permission to dream." I have experienced these things, and my confidence and trust in God has increased as I have had more encounters with Him. These "meetings" have been everywhere. I have met God while worshiping at church and at home. I have been with Him meaningfully when I have followed His impression to call someone to just hear how they are or make plans for getting together. I listen and He directs. I ask and He answers. I learned some time ago to not box God into doing things how I think He should respond. I have become open-ended with how God chooses to lead and direct my path. I have His Spirit in me so there is discernment to recognize His leadership, so I don't go off following anything that comes along. And as Jeremiah 29:11 states, His plans are only for my good, never evil. Since God is not in a box, neither am I.

Some others would like to think that they can confine me to one way of being or living. I am free. Free to dream and *dream big*! The sky is not the limit with my Father and me. No limits, no boundaries when it come to the possibilities ahead. This is called favor, and that is what He has for each of us. And the more we let go of controlling everything and everyone around us, the more we come closer to Him. The greater the favor manifests in our lives, the more evidence of His presence. I cannot tell you how many times His favor has practically been demonstrated in my life with provisions for my needs and those around me. The favor directed at me splashes on to others. I love to see this. The overflow of abundance and the looks on people's faces when they see His goodness are beautiful. I want to experience that again and again. This makes the time invested in intimacy so worth it when He showers His love on us.

His "intentions become my identity." What God intends is that I walk around "in the full knowledge and permission of the Father," just like Jesus did. Jesus knew exactly who He was and never denied His own identity. Knowing who He really was filled Him with the confidence to "do what He saw the Father doing and say what the Father was saying." Jesus is my model and example. I want to be that close and intimate with the Father that there is no doubt about who I am and can be. And the Father declares my identity joyfully. Just as I grew in knowledge and understanding of my family and ancestors to get a sense of my natural identity, I grow and mature in the knowledge and understanding of who I am to God and how He sees me. This is my spiritual and eternal identity and how I am known in Heaven. Adversities and challenges may come along the way, but nothing can "unseat me from wild favor." These events will only make me stronger and even more capable of overcoming anything in the future.

I must "see myself as His beloved" because that's what I am. This is not because of my performance or anything I could do to deserve or earn it. I am His much-beloved child because He chooses to see me that way. The Father has placed me in Christ so that all Jesus is I am too. Every favor, privilege, power, and authority are mine. This is not an ego trip anymore that any prince or princess on earth who lives in the benefits of being related to the monarch. To have that relationship, they only had to be born. All of us who have responded to the free love offered by God have been birthed into His kingdom and are now coheirs with Jesus in that realm. This sounds outlandish but it's true. Almost too good to be true. Its simplicity is sometimes what makes it so hard to grasp; yet, it is simple enough for a child to understand. Sometimes we adults try to make thing so hard and complicated. We are so performance based. But I cannot do or say or think anything enough to earn what God gives freely to those who will receive His love.

We get caught up and are "governed by past failures and events." All that stuff was taken care of, and the penalty for all of it was paid by Jesus. He paid it all. That's how great God's love is for us in that while we were still His enemies and rebellious against Him, Christ died for us. Jesus completely identified with our condition so that we could totally identify with His victory. "Joy, thanksgiving and rejoicing are the means by which we will both access and appropriate His desire" and intention for us. As I have grown and become more convinced of His desire and intention for me, I have developed and blossomed at an accelerated rate. Insight and understanding have increased. Love and care for others has opened up wonderful connections and relationships. I do not live in an outward Eden. There are still challenges and hurdles to overcome, but they are not consuming as they once were. There is a greater hope and confidence because He has shown Himself so strong, dependable, trustworthy, and abundant in all His dealings with me. I know from experience that these things will be only stepping-stones to my next upgrade, and there is always more.

From the second book, *Prophecy and Responsibility*, Cooke states that there is now a "season of Divine Acceleration." "There is a quickening Spirit upon your life." "The favor of the Lord is upon you to accelerate your development." This has absolutely been my experience. There has been more growth in the last eight years than in all the decades before. Time is being redeemed. There has been greater hunger and more intense desire to draw close to God. And He has certainly responded by coming closer to me. I have to learned to run and say yes much faster.

In the past, there have been centuries between the uttering of a prophetic word and its fulfillment. Even in the New Testament, fulfillment came faster than it had in the Old Testament. And now, two thousand years later, it is getting even faster. "Acceleration is a paradox. It is not always easy but it is hugely enjoyable." There is such delight to see and experience the revelation of some word and then see the completion come so quickly. This causes my faith to grow exponentially. I am part of the Healing Rooms and Sozo ministries at my church. The joy and fun that occurs when things happen in a matter of moments or a few days after praying for someone is exhilarating. This is my experience and it cannot be argued down. Some may ask, "What do you do when it doesn't happen quickly?" Keep on praying. Keep on pressing in. Keep calling things that are not as though they are. And we are not begging or pleading with God for these miracles; we are confident that we will see fulfillment eventually because He is good and He loves us. Ask and keep asking, knock and keep knocking, seek and keep seeking. We will get answers, have doors opened, and will find what we look for.

"Your heart will be overwhelmed with joy and laughter. Faith will rise up." Seeing manifestations of His presence are up to Him, not me. He is more interested in my faith being strong than I am. "I am giving you new eyes, a new heart, and a new mind. You will perceive totally differently. You will think like Me because I am elevating you to My level." This is the Lord's doing. I cannot do these things in and of myself. I just say yes and follow His leadership because I want all that He has for me. This usually comes when I do the opposite of what society and my culture tell me. "When you come into a situation that is resisting you, I want you to smile. I intend through the resistance to give you a double portion. I will increase the anointing (blessing) on you in those times." I know this. In the times of hard and difficult situations, I am not emotionally devastated like I used to be. When the challenges come, I no longer look to blame or chastise myself. I take it to my Father. We talk. I ask questions. He gives enlightenment and understanding, comfort and wisdom to see things from His perspective. This is radically different from how I once took the responsibility for everyone and everything around me. I take it all to Him now, and He shows me how to "cast all my cares on Him because He cares for me." By this, I "completely lose the ability to worry or be anxious."

In God's economy, when I have come through something to victory, He brings others across my path who are going through the same thing so that I can share what he has done for me and can do for them. "Each one reach one." This is how I truly know who I am. I know my identity and my inheritance. In this position of confidence, I will be able to be about my Father's business and disperse the favor over my life to others. In that way "every obstacle becomes an opportunity." It is His will for me (and us) that we know Him—personally and intimately—and that we be strong and do even greater things than Jesus did. "I will turn you into a different woman, then we will really get on with My business. I will do something so compelling, so wonderful, that I will make you a challenger against the enemy for the rest of your life." *Yes!* That's what I want. I want to overcome and help others into victory also. I want to triumph over all that seeks to tie me down. I will be free and will help others be free.

The third book, *Prophetic Wisdom*, has a word about inheritance and glory. I know what it is to be in someone's will and receive an inheritance. I receive the benefits because of the relationship. And even that was not by my choice. To be included in the will was the choice of the one who wrote it. They chose to benefit me because they included me in their family relations. They didn't have to but they did. My choice was whether I would receive that relational benefit or not. I could choose to reject it, but it would still be there available to me, waiting for my choice to receive what was designated as mine.

For many years, I was blinded by lies about God and myself that I did not see what was available to me. There were still times in my darkness that points of light would break through and brightness would come. God never gave up or quit trying with me. His Love is too passionate and relentless to quit. In coming to the end of my own fighting with God, I had to surrender to the idea that "it is My perception of you that must govern your heart." His opinion of me is the only one that matters because it is the only one that comes from complete knowledge and love for me. No one else; not even I can have an opinion as perfectly informed as God. He sees it all and still loves. "I have a huge heart for you; a mighty all-encompassing compassion for you." This is the provision He has for every one of us.

The more I open up and receive this love, the more I am drawn to the source of that love. I must be receptive to the benefits of relationship with God. The more I accept, the more there is. There is a limitless abundance. The only limitation is how much I am willing to receive. God has extravagant love with no bounds. This is what is available. Why did I go so long saying that He could not love me as relentlessly as He did? The only reason I did this was because I believed lies about God and myself. I have abandoned all that. I have stopped fighting and arguing. I am open to all that He has for me. Don't wait until your sixties to do this. It's never too late but spare yourself the agony of being an orphan when you are a much-loved child of the King.

We "occupy a high place in His affection." My response of acceptance is what releases the vastness of heaven to my benefit. "Grace can never be given in small doses. It can only be lavished." "It is fully received when my encounter with God fully exposes my life to unparalleled and unprecedented favor." *Wow!* This is for me? Really? *Yes!* This is who I am and what I have. The ocean full of grace is what opens the door for me to live in a growing atmosphere of permission to be all that He intends for me to be and have. When the battle and challenges of life come, He makes me an overcomer. But "a conqueror does more that survive the battle, they prosper in the fight. They do not just keep themselves free; they rescue people around them." I am allowed and must develop the mindset that says, "I cannot fail because I am amazingly loved." I must see myself as God sees me. This is radical! This is so opposite to the world view. The overflow of abundance is tied to how I see myself. If I think I am just a worm, God will still love me, but I will not be capable of receiving all that He has for me. I must see like God sees. This is exactly what He want to do in and for us. He wants to give us His perspective, but He can't if we refuse to accept it. Duh!

Why don't we receive it? We have believed lies that we're not good enough, we're not deserving, we've done too much wrong to get this love and abundance. *Ha!* This is a free gift! We can't earn it. We just have to receive it. We must agree with God about who He is and who we are. Stop arguing already! We can "boldly ask for our inheritance" because when we do that it means we finally know who we really are. "Your inheritance is incremental, tied to the ongoing calling and identity that I am showing you." God is passionately interested in us getting our inheritance. He relentlessly wants us to live in the fullness of our relationship with Him. He is "drawing us out of mediocrity into a deluge of His Spirit."

Just like the Roman centurion told Jesus that He did not need to go to his house to heal a sick person. He understood the authority that Jesus had. He knew that Jesus could speak, and it would be done. *Wow!* The centurion had a perfect understanding of identity. So Jesus spoke and the person was healed. The centurion's acceptance of what was available opened the door for the power to flow. We can do the same thing. By accepting what God can do for us and through us, we open the way for the flow of His limitless abundance. And because we are His much-loved children, He will do abundantly more than what we think or ask. He wants to lavish on us. And in the process, that abundance gets splashed on those around us. That's just how generous He is. He wants me and all His children to walk in the benefit of the identity we have so that others can be blessed. This is how the kingdom is spread—His children dispersing the blessings of that relationship to everyone. Then they can become open to a relationship with God and be distributors themselves. This is the kingdom's way! I want to be in this. I can't think of anything more fulfilling and satisfying. Let's do it! Let's be about our Father's business!

Get into a church atmosphere where prophecy is taught and encouraged. God still speaks to all His children and has plenty to say. You cannot do this alone. Get with others who are listening responsibly to God's voice. Write down some words that have been brought to your attention in reading the Bible or preaching or songs. Start listening to prophet's life, Graham Cooke and Bill Johnson, Steve Backlund, David Crone, Lana Vawser, and many more. The Spirit will guide you into truth and there is wisdom in the wealth of counselors.

CONCLUSION

This is not an end but a beginning or a step farther down the path of our journey. There can be no end because God is limitless. I know that's hard to wrap our minds around but it's the truth. There is so much more. We live in a very goal-oriented society. Achievement is the standard we are judged by and judge others. We have lost the concept that the journey to anything is part of the excitement and growth. There are many things in this life through which we must progress and grow. That process builds us physically and mentally, not just for our goals but also for other situations. How many times have we heard from a star athlete that their coach worked them physically hard but also instilled them with discipline and focus? When their career in the sports world was over, they still had the drive, ambition, and tools to succeed in other endeavors. This is what the Spirit does in us. We are taught and guided and helped through circumstances that challenge us but also strengthen us.

When these things happen, God provides the way to overcome and be better after it's done. We have accomplished something that will have perpetual benefit to ourselves and others. This is God's way of turning what others meant for our harm into something that results in victory and confidence for the next challenge. Jesus told us in John 16:33, "In the world you will have trouble. But have courage! I have overcome the world." There's that "heart" word again—*courage*. Do not fall in despair like someone who has no hope. *Arise!* Jesus has already won the war. And the Spirit that raised Him from the dead lives in all His children.

Tears have been a large part of my life. Since there were so many funerals in my young life, I shed many. I cried about pain, abandonment, and loneliness. At a few times in my life, tears were changed.

When I was an exchange student in Japan in my senior year of college, I came to the awareness that there were people who were born, lived, and died never having heard of the love that God had for them or of what Jesus had done for them. This was the first time I cried for people who did not know Him.

While in Iowa, a Christian woman became my friend. We would talk about the Lord and what He had done for us and in us. One day while sitting in my minivan with her, I began to weep in realization of the depth, purity, and power of His love for me. I had never experienced that before. It was very healing because it seemed to be coming from very deep hurts being touched and healed. Now it's not difficult or surprising at all for tears to flow in response to focusing on His love for me. The last part of Revelation 7:17 speaks to me:

And God will wipe all tears from their eyes.

I can picture all the people in white robes around the throne, ministering to God and the Lamb. He guides them to the springs of life and wipes away their tears. Someday I will have deeper and more exuberant experiences in His Love. There flowing tears will only be in Joy and Exaltation in Glory. For now, my tears are testimony to how wonderful and great He is to love someone like me. But...He does and I can never thank Him enough.

If you have already accepted the Love that God has offered you, start walking in the power that is also yours. You are a much-loved child of the Most High. Live like it! If you have not yet accepted this free gift of love and mercy, what is holding you back? Are you dealing with lies and accusations, judgements and condemnations? Please know that none of those are from God. He does not condemn the ones that He sent Jesus to die for. He couldn't do that. There is nothing in His character or nature to deny any good thing to His precious children. But He will not force Himself on anyone. He respects our freedom to choose. If there were no choice, there would be no freedom.

Please receive the love and healing He has for you. When you do, you will find out that there is so much available to you—like what has been described in this book. God's intention and desire is for you to be all that He made you to be. His plan is for you to have a powerful and meaningful relationship with Him so that you can grow into a son or daughter who can be about their Father's business—changing atmospheres and lives. This is the kingdom, and this is what is available to everyone. God loved everyone so much that He sent Jesus to demonstrate that love.

Whoever would believe and receive that love would eternally live in fellowship with God and never be separated from the source of life (based on John 3:16). This is what is offered to everyone. Once that relationship is established, the adventure begins. The Spirit of God is given to us to guide us into truth. The Spirit is brilliant at this. This is His joy and delight to comfort, nurture, and guide us into all that God has for us. This is the way of daily living and growing more like Jesus. But we're not cut out of cookie molds. We are each unique expressions of the multifaceted God. His has given us gifts and talents special for each one. We get to explore the path He has prepared for us especially. God does not love us all the same. He loves us all uniquely. He revels in each individual and their life expression. This is such a radical view. The world view is that we are nothing special. Just another cog on the wheel. We're just accidents that happened to pop out of the primordial ooze.

We're all the same. Nothing could be further from the truth. We *are* special and unique. He made us that way. God does not want mindless robots. He wants a family of individuals with elaborate diversities. Some religious groups don't like this and even fear it. However, God's love is for them also, and it is the Spirit's job to lead them into truth if they will open to His leadership. Don't be hard as stone. "I will give you a new heart and put a new Spirit within you. I will take the heart of stone from your body and give you a heart of soft, supple flesh. I will put My Spirit inside you so you can follow My Directions," Ezekiel 36:26–27. Stubbornness doesn't get us anywhere, and it only perpetuates the lie that we know better than God and don't need Him anyway. None of us knows better. Look at the mess this world is in right now to see that. Through it all, God still loves us and wants the best for us one at a time individually. And He has a purpose for each of His children to spread that kingdom love one life at a time until the whole earth is filled with that glorious truth. If someone is in need or suffering, God directs His children to release His goodness to those situations. Not every need has been met yet but neither has everyone who calls themself a child of God stood up to be about the Father's business. There is plenty to do, and we must know who we are so that we will be empowered to make a difference to those around us. My prayer is that you would get to know who you really are and who God is for you because the world is aching and groaning for us to step in and change things like only sons and daughter of the Most High can. *Join me! Let's do it!*

ABOUT THE AUTHOR

Melody Bahr is a mother and grandmother. She is a trained musician and teacher. She was also a preacher's kid and an army brat. She was born in Waco, Texas, and at twenty-two months, traveled with her family to Germany to join her father who was a Chaplin stationed there. After a few years, she returned to the US and lived in Rolla, Missouri. In 1960, she moved back to Texas and lived in Austin with her mother. After graduating from Crockett High School ('70) in south Austin, she went to Baylor University. After finishing ('75), she attended Southwestern Baptist Theological Seminary in Fort Worth, Texas.

She was married in 1978. When they both finished seminary, they moved to the Rio Grande Valley for eight years. Her next move took the family to Iowa where they lived for nineteen years. While in Iowa, she worked for the DOT as an examiner at a driver's license station in Davenport for twelve years. In 2010, she returned to Texas with family and lives there now. She has two smart and beautiful grown daughters who have blessed her with two smart and beautiful grandchildren. She is very active in family activities and in her church, True Life Fellowship.

CPSIA information can be obtained
at www.ICGtesting.com
Printed in the USA
FSHW010329110820
72849FS

9 781644 680896